Servant
Ministry

Text copyright © Tony Horsfall 2013
The author asserts the moral right
to be identified as the author of this work

Published by
The Bible Reading Fellowship
15 The Chambers, Vineyard
Abingdon OX14 3FE
United Kingdom
Tel: +44 (0)1865 319700
Email: enquiries@brf.org.uk
Website: www.brf.org.uk
BRF is a Registered Charity

ISBN 978 0 85746 088 2

First published 2013

10 9 8 7 6 5 4 3 2 1 0

Acknowledgments
Unless otherwise stated, scripture quotations are taken from the Holy Bible, New International
Version (Anglicised edition), copyright © 1979, 1984, 2011 by Biblica (formerly International
Bible Society), and are used by permission of Hodder & Stoughton Publishers, an Hachett UK
company. All rights reserved. 'NIV' is a registered trademark of Biblica (formerly International
Bible Society). UK trademark number 1448790.

Extracts from the Authorised Version of the Bible (The King James Bible), the rights in which
are vested in the Crown, are reproduced by permission of the Crown's Patentee, Cambridge
University Press.

Scripture quotations from THE MESSAGE. Copyright © by Eugene H. Peterson 193, 1994, 1995.
Used by permission of NavPress Publishing Group.

The paper used in the production of this publication was supplied by mills that source their
raw materials from sustainably managed forests. Soy-based inks were used in its printing and
the laminate film is biodegradable.

A catalogue record for this book is available from the British Library

Printed in Singapore by Craft Print International Ltd

Servant
Ministry

A portrait of Christ and a pattern
for his followers

TONY HORSFALL

To Rennis Ponniah,
Anglican Bishop of Singapore.

It is a privilege to know you, dear brother,
and count you as a friend. I know this passage of
scripture is one that you love. I also know it is one that
you exemplify in your ministry, for you are
a true servant leader.

May God continue to enable you
and grace you with his presence
as you lead his people
in the footsteps of Jesus.

Contents

'Here is my servant, whom I uphold,
my chosen one in whom I delight;
I will put my Spirit on him,
and he will bring justice to the nations.
He will not shout or cry out,
or raise his voice in the streets.
A bruised reed he will not break,
and a smouldering wick he will not snuff out.
In faithfulness he will bring forth justice;
he will not falter or be discouraged
till he establishes justice on earth.
In his teaching the islands will put their hope.'

This is what God the Lord says—
the Creator of the heavens, who stretches them out,
who spreads out the earth with all that springs from it,
who gives breath to its people,
and life to those who walk on it:
'I, the Lord, have called you in righteousness;
I will take hold of your hand.
I will keep you and will make you
to be a covenant for the people
and a light for the Gentiles,
to open eyes that are blind,
to free captives from prison
and to release from the dungeon those who sit in darkness.

'I am the Lord; that is my name!
I will not yield my glory to another
or my praise to idols.
See, the former things have taken place,
and new things I declare;
before they spring into being
I announce them to you.'
ISAIAH 42:1–9

6

Foreword

In September 2010 Tony Horsfall led a staff retreat at Redcliffe College. The retreat was called 'Time to Stop', but it took place about five days before the students started arriving, so we didn't really have time to stop! However, his focus on our identity and purpose, and his unpacking of the resources available to us, allowed us, individually and corporately, to remember during that particularly challenging year, to stop, reflect and re-engage in God's service.

This book presents a truly biblical view of servanthood—not like being some kind of benign auntie for whom nothing is too much trouble but, rather, being called to live as God intends us to live. I teach a postgraduate class on leadership and I sometimes tell the students that I get fed up with talk of 'servant leadership', partly because I see many other scriptural metaphors for leadership but also because I think Christians have misunderstood servant leadership and servanthood generally. Tony, however, has not.

God intends us to live and serve in security. Tony starts with identity and calling. This is vital. We need to know who we are: both our frailty and our status as children of the living God, loved by a Father who delights in his children. He goes on to justice and compassion—two concepts that Christian writers often find hard to hold in tension. Tony, however, does not.

God intends us to live confidently. Servants serve a master (in our case, the Lord), not just every person we bump into. Knowing how God wants us to serve him in each and every situation—whether it demands compassion or righteous anger, clear leadership or wise counsel—is vital to effective Christian living. To be able to do it in confidence because we know who we are, and who we are called to be, allows us to serve effectively.

Tony has served the church so well in the writing of this book. It has the potential to make the church a better bride of Christ and each individual Christian a closer reflection of Jesus this side of heaven.

Rob Hay, Principal, Redcliffe College

Introduction

My computer has a problem with the word 'servanthood'. It does not recognise it. Every time I use the word, the computer underlines it in red, suggesting it is wrong in some way, but it offers no alternative. Likewise, my home dictionary has no reference to servanthood. I was beginning to think I had made it up until, much to my relief, a quick check on the internet showed that lots of other people also use the word. It does exist.

Even so, it is difficult to find an exact definition, so I have made up my own. Servanthood is the state of being a servant; the attitude of mind, disposition of heart and daily practice of someone who serves. Since this is a book about servanthood, it is important to be sure from the outset that it is a valid word!

Servant Ministry is based on the first Servant Song in Isaiah (42:1–9) and could be described as a practical exposition of this passage. My intention is to explain the meaning of the text and then to apply its teaching to the biblical theme of servanthood. It will lead us quite naturally to explore some significant topics: the motivation for service and the call to serve; valid expressions of servanthood and the link between evangelism and social action; character formation and what it means to be a servant, especially in leadership; how to sustain ourselves over the long haul in the harsh realities of ministry; the importance of listening to God and being directed by him in what we do, both on a daily basis and over the course of a lifetime.

My basic assumption throughout is that servanthood is for all believers, not just for those in some form of 'full-time' ministry, and I hope this comes across clearly because it is vital for the health and vitality of local churches that every member appreciates and understands his or her role as a servant of God. At the same time, my focus will be on those in Christian leadership and cross-cultural ministry for whom the call to serve has led to significant life changes that impact them on a daily basis. Inevitably we will cover the topic of servant leadership, and I hope we might grasp the principles behind it in a fresh way while avoiding some of the common misconceptions and distortions. It is my strong conviction that servant leadership is vital for the well-being and effectiveness of any church or Christian organisation in the 21st century. For me, Christian leadership is synonymous with servant leadership.

We will approach the Servant Song through two lenses, seeing it first of all as a portrait of Christ and secondly as a pattern for his followers. Jesus shows us through his life on earth what it means to be a servant, and he perfectly fulfils the picture painted for us in Isaiah. He is an example to us of true servanthood, and we are called with God's help to imitate him: 'Whoever claims to live in him must walk as Jesus did' (1 John 2:6). Servanthood can never be an optional extra in the Christian life; it is its foundation stone, and all disciples of Jesus must see themselves as servants. Peter says it clearly: 'Live as free persons, but do not use your freedom as a cover up for evil; live as servants of God' (1 Peter 2:16, NIV 1984).

Readers who are familiar with my earlier books may think that the theme of servanthood is a departure from my usual emphasis, since it is about action rather than reflection, doing rather than being. I see it more as a natural progression, because the reflective life that I so often espouse is valid only if it is expressed outwardly in tangible acts of service, and love for God is real only when it leads to love for others. *Servant Ministry* should therefore be an excellent follow-up to *Working from a Place of Rest* (BRF, 2010). Many of the themes I have previously written about will occur here but in a less prominent way. Servanthood assumes that we have a strong inner life, that we are secure in God's love and that we know how to allow God to work in us and through us.

Read the chapters slowly and carefully, ponder the words and meditate on the scriptures that you read. My prayer is that as you interact with these pages, you will meet with God in a fresh way and will be drawn into a deeper place of love and appreciation for Jesus, which will be expressed in joyful service to God and others.

The Servant's Identity

1

Behold my servant

Here is my servant, whom I uphold.
ISAIAH 42:1

'Look this way, children.'

I'm sure we can all remember moments from our childhood when the teacher stood before us and tried to gain our attention. Children's minds wander so easily and learning can take place only when we are fully focused and concentrating on the matter in hand. Therefore, it is a natural and essential first step in the learning process when the teacher calls for the attention of the class and, often with a clap of the hands, invites them to look in her direction.

The first of the Servant Songs in Isaiah begins with a similar summons to attentiveness: 'Here is my servant, whom I uphold, my chosen one in whom I delight.' We are called to turn from what we are doing and to take note of the person who is being introduced to us. It is an important moment, for we are being invited to meet a very special person, at least in the eyes of God—the servant of the Lord.

It was the German Lutheran scholar Bernhard Duhm who first identified the four Servant Songs and sparked so much interest in these passages. In his 1892 commentary on Isaiah he suggested that the sections 42:1–9; 49:1–6; 50:4–9 and 52:13—53:12 stood apart because of their lyrical character and their focus on an unidentified 'servant' figure. Much debate has since followed, and various interpretations of these passages have been given over the years in order to identify the servant.

An obvious starting point is to suggest that Isaiah is referring to himself in his role as a prophet to Israel, and he is indeed described by God as 'my servant Isaiah' (20:3), but there are too many details in the songs that do not fit his profile. The role described in the songs seems to be too large for him and has a future perspective about it, indicating someone still to appear.

A second popular interpretation suggests that the nation of Israel is in mind, again with good reason. Israel was brought into being for the purpose of serving God, and Isaiah bears witness to this high calling: 'He said to me, "You are my servant, Israel, in whom I will display my splendour"' (49:3). However, Israel by and large did not fulfil this calling and was often rebellious and wayward, whereas the servant is portrayed as one who gives perfect obedience and is faithful to God. Furthermore, it seems to be an individual who is in mind, one who suffers vicariously for others (as in 53:4–5) and brings healing through his death. Israel does not fully fit the description of this particular servant.

Not surprisingly, many commentators have seen a glimpse of the coming Messiah, an individual who will fulfil all that Israel was meant to be. Through his obedience and undeserved suffering, he brings blessing to many, but remains anonymous in these passages. Without doubt, we are now moving along the right lines as we seek an understanding of the person of the servant.

It is only when we begin to read the New Testament that the pieces of the jigsaw finally fall into place and we can see the servant's true identity. These verses speak directly of Jesus of Nazareth. He is the servant described there, and he is the one upon whom we are called to focus our attention.

Matthew, writing as a Jew for a Jewish audience, has no hesitation in applying these scriptures to Jesus and seeing their outworking in Jesus' life and ministry. He writes, 'This was to fulfil what was spoken through the prophet Isaiah,' and then quotes extensively from Isaiah 42:1–4, showing Jesus to be the servant (see Matthew 12:17–21). Likewise, when Philip meets the Ethiopian official riding in his chariot on the Gaza road and reading from Isaiah 53, he has no reservation in identifying Jesus as the suffering servant.

'Tell me, please, who is the prophet talking about, himself or someone else?' asks the Ethiopian (Acts 8:34). 'Then Philip began with that very passage of Scripture and told him the good news about Jesus' (v. 35). The apostles and the first believers seem to have been in no doubt about the servant's identity: it was Jesus, the one they loved to call 'your holy servant' (Acts 4:27, 30).

To further confirm this identification, Jesus clearly saw himself in the role of the servant, both towards the Father who had sent him and towards those he came to save: 'For even the Son of Man did not come to be served, but to serve, and to give his life as a ransom for many' (Mark 10:45). The amazing parallels between the suffering servant described in Isaiah 53 and the death of Jesus at Calvary reinforce this conclusion. No one else could possibly have been in mind, for no one else suffered in the way he did, in obvious fulfilment of the scriptures.

The NIV is rather bland and low-key in its translation of Isaiah 42:1. 'Here is my servant' somehow suggests a take-it-or-leave-it attitude—a kind of 'you may be interested in this; then again, you may not' approach. I much prefer the older translations that use a great Bible word: 'Behold!' (KJV). That really is a summons and a call to pay attention. It says 'Hold before you' what you are about to see, because it is important and significant and deserves your utmost concentration and careful scrutiny.

Why? Because here we are presented with a portrait of the servant, painted for us by God himself. It is almost as if the Father stands before us and, with pride and satisfaction, says to us, 'Have you seen my Son?' We can feel the delight that he has in the Son's willingness to take upon himself the role of the servant and to do the Father's will, and he wants to share his pleasure with everyone.

This book is primarily a devotional book. I hope it will inform your mind (helping you to develop a servant attitude) and challenge your will (moving you to act in servant ways), but ideally I want it to touch your heart and cause you to worship the one who is the true servant of God. Therefore, as you begin to read, I suggest you take a few moments to behold the Son who is a servant.

- To behold is to *see*, to notice, to observe, to give your full attention to something. Consciously turn your inward gaze towards Jesus, resting the eyes of your heart upon him. The writer to the Hebrews says, 'Let us fix our eyes on Jesus, the author and perfecter of our faith' (Hebrews 12:2). If your eyes have wandered and your gaze has been elsewhere, or if your life has become fragmented and scattered, gently refocus yourself upon him. If you have been rushing and hurrying, busy with this and that, pause for a moment and slow down. Let him become the centre of your attention once again.
- To behold is to *study*, to appreciate, to meditate upon. Allow your mind to think deeply about what you read in this Servant Song, and reflect on what you discover about Jesus, as an expert might study a work of art, for this is a portrait in words painted by the Holy Spirit. Ponder the truths that are revealed to you and let them slip from your mind to your heart, taking hold of you in your innermost being until they become part of you and transform you. It is by beholding him that we are changed into his likeness (2 Corinthians 3:18), so take time to linger and to browse. Allow his portrait to become your pattern.
- To behold is to *gaze* with loving attentiveness, to worship, to adore. If we see Jesus in the beauty of who he is as a person, we will be captivated by him. No one who sees him as the willing and obedient servant, the humble one who comes gladly and submissively to do the Father's will or the suffering one who gives his innocent life in place of sinful men and women, can fail to be moved to love him in return. This is the heart of contemplation, and, before we begin to follow in his footsteps and move into a life of service of our own, we must first bow the knee in humble adoration. Do not be afraid to enter the temple of your heart and, like King David of old, 'behold the beauty of the Lord' (Psalm 27:4, KJV).

2

Emptied and humbled

Here is my servant, whom I uphold, my chosen one in whom I delight.
ISAIAH 42:1

British people love costume drama. We like nothing better than to be transported back to days gone by, when men behaved like gentlemen, ladies dressed elegantly, people spoke correctly and all was well with the world (or so we imagine). In particular, we enjoy period stories about the upper classes—films like *Pride & Prejudice* and *Sense & Sensibility*, or TV shows like *Upstairs, Downstairs* and *Downton Abbey*.

It isn't that we want to return to those days and restore the class system. We idealise them deliberately because they provide a brief escape from the social chaos of our world, but no one today would want to be a servant and live 'downstairs'. My mother was born in 1915 and, like many young girls of her generation, went 'into service' after leaving school. She worked as a maid for a doctor's family and, while it may have provided her with a good domestic training, it was not something she wanted her daughters to take up. She was only too glad to leave and find her freedom again.

How we think about servanthood, and being a servant, is culturally conditioned. In some cultures, to serve other people is an honour and there is pleasure and delight in being able to help or give assistance. Service is offered cheerfully, with a smile, and brings its own reward. In other cultures (and I include my own), being a servant is viewed negatively as the lowest rung on the employment ladder. Service roles are increasingly seen as degrading, to be avoided or left to others, and, when service is offered, it is given grudgingly and with reluctance. There is a fear of being taken advantage of and a sense that it is demeaning, so serving others is endured rather than enjoyed.

What seems amazing to some of us, therefore, is that the Son of God came into our world as a servant. 'Here is my servant,' says Isaiah 42:1. He came to serve his Father, having been sent into the world to do the Father's will. A servant is one who lives to do the will of another. Jesus fully fitted that description, and did so gladly and without any reluctance. The writer to the Hebrews takes some Old Testament words (Psalm 40:6–8) and puts them into the mouth of Jesus to emphasise this very point:

Therefore, when Christ came into the world, he said: 'Sacrifice and offering you did not desire, but a body you prepared for me; with burnt offerings and sin offerings you were not pleased. Then I said, "Here I am—it is written about me in the scroll—I have come to do your will, O God."' (Hebrews 10:5–7)

What we notice, first, is the absolute willingness of the Son to step into the servant's role and to live to please the Father. This was his destiny and he accepted it joyfully. He came into the world for one purpose only, to do the Father's will. Second, we see that the incarnation was intended to enable him to do this very thing. In the miracle of what we call the virgin birth, the Son of God was given a human body as the means through which he would accomplish the will of God. At the heart of the Father's purpose in sending his Son was the prospect of our salvation, a salvation that would require the Son to lay down his life as a once-for-all-time sacrifice for sin. It was always written into the job description of the servant that he would be a *suffering* servant, and from this task the Son never flinched, such was the level of his obedience.

So, when the Son of God entered our world, he took upon himself the form of a servant—and this was not just window-dressing. He did not simply take to himself the garments of a servant and play a part, as children do when they play 'dressing up'. No, he became a servant at the core of his being, and this amazing transformation is described in detail for us in the Christological hymn in Philippians 2:5–11:

Your attitude should be the same as that of Christ Jesus: Who, being in very nature God, did not consider equality with God something to be grasped, but made himself nothing, taking the very nature of a servant, being made in human likeness. And being found in appearance as a man, he humbled himself and became obedient to death—even death on a cross!' (vv. 5–8)

As we read these beautiful words on servanthood, two phrases stand out as being indicative of what it meant for the Son of God to walk this downward way: first he made himself nothing (v. 7, literally 'emptied himself'), and then he humbled himself (v. 8).

Some theologians are nervous around the word 'emptied' because they fear that in describing the glory that the Son laid aside in being born as a man, we might surrender his divinity, but that need not be the case. Jesus remained fully God but, in becoming fully man, it was necessary for him to let go of some of the privileges and prerogatives he enjoyed as God. Elsewhere, Paul expresses it like this: 'For you know the grace of our Lord Jesus Christ, that though he was rich, yet for your sakes he became poor, so that you through his poverty might become rich' (2 Corinthians 8:9). Clearly, then, something of significance was given up as he moved from heaven to earth. He left behind the status, honour, worship and adoration that were his by right, exchanging them for the obscurity and vulnerability of birth in a cattle shed.

This emptying is really all about an attitude of heart and mind, an attitude of selflessness that makes it possible for someone to let go of something precious in order to serve another and achieve a higher good. The Son did not cling to the place of equality with God with the tenacity of a person holding on to something for dear life—such as a handbag being grabbed by a snatch-thief. No, he willingly released from his grip all his personal rights as God in order to fulfil the Father's will. He came into the world empty-handed. Here is the heart of servanthood—the selfless giving of oneself to meet the need of others, even at personal cost.

The Son was born in true human likeness. The omnipresent one was now confined to a human body in a manger; the omnipotent one was now dependent on others to feed and clothe him; the omniscient one now learned to walk and talk, to read and write. As he grew older, he matured physically, moving from baby to boy, from adolescent to full-grown man, subject to all the normal laws of growth and development. When he passed down the street, he looked and sounded like everyone else. There were no distinguishing physical marks, no 'holy glow' that drew attention to him; he came 'incognito'. He was found in appearance as an ordinary Jewish man, and his humanity was his servant's robe.

Yet there were more steps on the servant's downward path. After selflessness, humility is the second distinguishing mark of a servant, and we can see how the Son was called upon to humble himself, submitting himself to the Father's will. As he lived his life, he made God known through his teaching and by his ways, for this was one of the reasons why he came: 'Anyone who has seen me has seen the Father,' he said (John 14:9). He was careful to do and say only those things that the Father commanded him, never acting independently but always being led by God: 'For I did not speak of my own accord, but the Father who sent me commanded me what to say and how to say it' (12:49). Like a true servant, his eyes were always upon his Master, waiting for a word of instruction or to anticipate a need or desire (Psalm 123:2).

Eventually the time came when he was called to move towards the cross, when the step of obedience would lead even lower, to the place of death, and he would humbly place himself in the hands of cruel men. The struggle for obedience to the ultimate sacrifice was real but never in doubt: 'The reason my Father loves me is that I lay down my life—only to take it up again. No one takes it from me, but I lay it down of my own accord. I have authority to lay it down and authority to take it up again. This command I received from my

Father' (John 10:17–18). There was a choice, of course, played out in the agony of the garden of Gethsemane (Mark 14:32–36), when his real humanity screamed out for release, but there was only one way he was ever going to go: 'Yet not what I will, but what you will' was etched upon his soul (v. 36).

So, like a lamb led to the slaughter, he gave himself to everything the world, in its hatred of God, could throw at him—trumped-up charges and biased verdicts, intimidation and physical abuse, scorn and humiliation, beating and imprisonment, the desertion of his friends and the rejection of his people, and finally the scandal of the cross. He was nailed and pierced, brutalised and abandoned, stripped naked and hung up to die in public like a common criminal. To all this he submitted himself in great humility as he became 'obedient to death'.

Why? Because, in the mystery of redemption and the need for atonement, it was the will of the Lord to bruise him (Isaiah 53:10). There on the cross, the one who had no sin was made to be sin (taking upon himself the sin of the whole world) so that we might become the righteousness of God—that is, be forgiven and made acceptable again to God (see 2 Corinthians 5:21). In this great act of salvation he was serving not only his Father but us as well, for it was by dying in our place that he enabled us to be forgiven and reconciled to God. His sacrificial death was the ransom that set us free (Mark 10:45).

The work of the servant having been accomplished at Calvary, God then brought him to life again in the triumph of the resurrection, as the Christological hymn goes on to make clear: 'Therefore God exalted him...' (Philippians 2:9). Humiliation leads to exaltation, for, in spiritual terms, the way up is always the way down. There is no other way. This is the path that the true servant walked, and everyone who follows in his footsteps will be called to a life of selfless service and humble obedience to God—but always in the knowledge that the way of the cross leads to life.

It is interesting to see how Paul uses this passage about the downward way of Jesus within the Philippian letter as a whole. One of his reasons for writing seems to have been to encourage two of his prominent fellow workers, Euodia and Syntyche, to patch up their differences (Philippians 4:2). This may explain why he uses the Christological hymn, because it is prefaced by a call to humility in relationships: 'Do nothing out of selfish ambition or vain conceit, but in humility consider others better than yourselves. Each of you should look not only to your own interests, but also to the interests of others' (2:3–4). Such behaviour is possible only if God's people have adopted the mind of Christ displayed in his giving up of personal rights and adopting a humble approach. A servant heart is essential in the tricky business of interpersonal relationships, even in the church.

To add weight to his argument, Paul then mentions his son in the faith, Timothy, who will soon be arriving in Philippi. Timothy has been in a mentoring relationship with Paul, and it is clear that servanthood is something that has been stressed. He has now become a living example of the principles that Paul has been speaking about: 'I have no one else like him,' Paul says, 'who takes a genuine interest in your welfare. For everyone looks out for his own interests, not those of Jesus Christ' (2:20–21). Here is a young man who has grasped what it is all about, who has learned how to live outside of himself and is able, when necessary, to place the needs of others before his own.

Timothy will model servanthood for the Philippians because he is a true follower of Jesus Christ, and only when believers (both then and now) learn to serve one another in love will the church really thrive. Jesus has led the way on the downward path and calls us to follow in his steps.

Reflection

- Meditate further on the way in which Jesus first 'emptied' himself at the manger and then 'humbled' himself at the cross.
- Think about ways in which you are called to be a servant, and consider your attitude towards servanthood.

3

Chosen and loved

Here is my servant, whom I uphold, my chosen one in whom I delight.
ISAIAH 42:1

In being introduced to the servant, we have been invited to pause to take a good long look at him. Our attention has been grabbed and we have begun to realise that this is no ordinary servant, to be despised and looked down upon. He has a noble calling and serves a noble Master. He brings with him not shame and disgrace but honour and dignity. He walks uprightly, with confidence and authority, because he comes as a representative of the Sovereign Lord. He is one to be emulated.

Through the words of the prophet, God points us to his servant, and we hear him given an amazing assurance as the one 'whom I uphold'. Here is a divinely stated guarantee that the servant will not fail in his task because he will be 'held up' (strengthened, supported, supplied, equipped) in whatever he undertakes for his Lord. All the resources of heaven will be at his disposal, and his feet will stand on solid ground. THE MESSAGE puts it like this: 'Take a good look at my servant. I'm backing him to the hilt.' There is no chance of his being sent on a mission and then forgotten about or being commissioned and then left to fend for himself. He serves with divine authorisation and everything he needs to do a good job will be given to him.

We will return to this thought of the servant's confidence later, as it recurs elsewhere in the song in more detail. Alongside the promise of support, though, the servant is given a further wonderful affirmation of the esteem in which he is held, in words again designed to strengthen him for the task: he is 'my chosen one in whom I delight'. There is no sense here that the servant is an unseen nobody, silently performing his duties and hidden from his Master's gaze. He is not despised or looked down upon or disregarded as inconsequential. No, the Master is aware of him, thinks highly of him and feels affection for him. This is communicated in words so that the servant may know it and may value himself and his calling.

The servant is the 'chosen one'. Here is a term that reminds us that a servant must be called to a particular task and set apart for a specific role. From this perspective, people like Abraham, David and Moses are all said to have been chosen (see Genesis 18:19; Psalm 89:3; 106:23). In God's service there are no volunteers (strange as that may seem!), only those appointed by God. This is brought out in Hebrews 5:4–5, where there is a discussion about the selection of the high priest: 'No one takes this honour upon himself; he must be called by God, just as Aaron was. So Christ did not take upon himself the glory of becoming a high priest.' Even Jesus did not volunteer! He was appointed by God to the role in which he now serves (as a merciful and faithful high priest). Likewise, he became the servant because he was chosen; this was the Father's will for him.

The reality of this chosenness came as a gradual realisation to the boy Jesus. His understanding of who he was and what he had come to do was an unfolding revelation, for, as we have seen, in his humanity he had to develop in normal ways. By the age of twelve he was already beginning to sense his divine destiny. He astounded the temple teachers with his wisdom and insight, and surprised his parents by reminding them that he must be 'about my Father's business' (Luke 2:49, KJV). Doubtless, as he grew older, this awareness grew stronger, coming to fulfilment in his baptism when he presented himself to the Father for the work he was called to do.

The word 'chosen' also contains a sense of affection and specialness. Only once in the Gospels is Jesus called the Chosen One. It is used rather scornfully during the crucifixion as a description of the 'so-called' Messiah (Luke 23:35). Peter, however, uses it quite positively, comparing Jesus to a living stone that the builders have rejected but, in God's sight, is chosen and precious, one that becomes the cornerstone of the building (see 1 Peter 2:4–8).

This sense of affection and appreciation for the servant naturally spills over into the words that follow: he is one 'in whom I delight'. When we look closely at the life of Jesus, we see how important it was for him to know that he was loved by the Father. He seems to have lived within the orbit of that love, and took his sense of identity from it. It was the motivation for his life of service, the source of his confidence and joy. The apostle John, the most intimate of his companions, highlights this in the fourth Gospel: 'The Father loves the Son and has placed everything in his hands' (John 3:35); 'For the Father loves the Son and shows him all he does' (5:20); 'As the Father has loved me, so have I loved you' (15:9); 'Father, I want those you have given me to be with me where I am, and to see my glory, the glory you have given me because you loved me before the creation of the world' (17:24).

Matthew also draws our attention to the Son's awareness of being loved by the Father. I have already mentioned how he quotes quite fully from the first Servant Song to describe the ministry of Jesus. In repeating Isaiah 42:1, however, Matthew makes a subtle change to the wording—which, I guess, under the inspiration of the Holy Spirit, he was allowed to do! His version omits the expression 'whom I uphold' and says this: 'Here is my servant whom I have chosen, *the one I love*, in whom I delight' (Matthew 12:18, my italics). Nothing could be plainer than that. No wonder, then, that Paul speaks of Jesus as being 'the One he loves' (Ephesians 1:6) and 'the Son he loves' (Colossians 1:13).

It was at his baptism that Jesus stepped on to the public stage in his ministry and consciously took upon himself the role of the servant. Not only did the Holy Spirit come upon him but a voice came from heaven, confirming him in his identity and calling out, 'This is my Son, whom I love; with him I am well pleased' (Matthew 3:17; see Mark 1:11; Luke 3:22). It is impossible not to see here an echo of Isaiah 42:1, the opening of the Servant Song. As he began his ministry, Jesus in his humanity needed to hear such powerful words of affirmation deep in his own soul, and to sense the presence of the Spirit empowering him for all that lay ahead. Notice, too, that this affirmation was given before he had done anything. The love of the Father was in no way conditional upon his performance or productivity.

In a similar way, shortly before he went to the cross, the Father spoke to him again on the mount of transfiguration. Out of the cloud a voice said, 'This is my Son, whom I love; with him I am well pleased. Listen to him!' (Matthew 17:5; see Mark 9:7; Luke 9:35). The other Gospel writers slightly vary the words they use on this occasion, but Matthew records exactly the same words as he did in his account of the baptism. Again, we sense the Father upholding his servant, strengthening him by words of reassurance at a crucial moment in his ministry. How important that must have been for him—and how important for his disciples to be reminded to listen to him!

We have dwelt at some length on the fact that the servant is made aware of his being loved, because genuine self-esteem is vital to true servanthood. Only those who know themselves to be loved can give the kind of love from which true service flows. Servanthood is not for those who demean themselves or consider themselves inferior to others, thinking that they must serve because they are worthless and deserve nothing better. Nor is it for those who feel unloved and think they will be appreciated more if they pamper to the needs and wishes of others, denying any needs of their own in order to bolster a fragile ego. No, servanthood in the biblical sense is for those who have a clear sense of their identity, who know they are loved by God and are aware of being called to a particular task; it is for the strong, not the weak.

One of the clearest demonstrations of the servant heart of Jesus is seen in his washing of the disciples' feet (John 13:1–17). They are about to celebrate the Passover meal together and are gathered in the upper room. Everything has been prepared for them and they are sitting around, sharing relaxed conversation. Only one thing is amiss. A bowl of water and a towel have been set out for the customary foot-washing, but there seems to be no household servant present to perform this menial task.

Then, to the surprise of everyone, Jesus stands up, takes off his outer garment and wraps the towel around himself in the manner (or 'form') of a servant. There is a moment of shocked silence as the disciples watch him take the bowl and begin to wash their dirty, dusty feet. They are embarrassed and ashamed, but Jesus has not acted in this way to show them up; it is an act of love on his part, and, because he has the attitude of a servant, it is a spontaneous response to an observed need. Status and position are no barrier to him in doing what needs to be done, however menial and lowly it may be.

Jesus is able to do this because he is secure in his relationship with the Father: 'Jesus knew that the Father had put all things under his power, and that he had come from God and was returning to God' (v. 3). This security provides the backdrop to his action, for he has no fear of losing face or reputation by serving others. Further, he can meet the needs of his disciples because he truly loves them: 'Having loved his own who were in the world, he now showed them the full extent of his love' (v. 1) His love for them was unending because it was actually the Father's love welling up within him. Knowing himself to be loved, he could love others freely and deeply—even the slow-to-learn disciples, and even his betrayer, Judas (whose feet he also washed). This is why I say that true servanthood is possible only when we are operating out of a strong sense of our own belovedness.

The washing of the disciples' feet provides the context for some important words about relationships. As Jesus prepares to return to the Father and send his disciples into the world, he wants them to know that, among his followers, servanthood is to be the norm: 'Now that I, your Lord and Teacher, have washed your feet, you also should wash one another's feet. I have set you an example that you should do as I have done for you' (vv. 14–15). This will be important for the future when the church comes into being, for Jesus is aware of the human tendency to want to get to the top and be served rather than to serve. By washing his disciples' feet he has not only modelled humility but also demonstrated true leadership. Real leadership is servant leadership. Power and authority are not to be exercised in a despotic way, but from a servant heart that seeks to benefit others and not burden them. As their Teacher and Lord, Jesus might well have asked them to wash his feet, but he chose rather to serve them. He did not exercise his rights but laid them aside (an echo of his original self-emptying).

Here is an example for the disciples of a principle that must undergird all Christian leadership: leaders must be willing to serve those they lead, even at personal cost. 'Do you understand what I have done for you?' Jesus asks (v. 12), and it is a pertinent question for us as well, for it points us to a style of leadership and interpersonal relationships that is alien to the world but expressive of the kingdom of God, where the humble serving of one another is a core value.

The washing of one another's feet is a custom still practised in some churches today, and I have experienced it myself among a group of mission partners in Singapore. It is a moving and disarming experience in itself, but what matters is what lies behind the action—the willingness to serve humbly, to become involved in the nitty-gritty of practical care for one another. 'Washing the feet of the saints', in the early church, became a synonym for showing hospitality and offering kindness, especially to strangers (1 Timothy 5:10). However we practise it, it will require a servant heart, and that is what makes Christian leadership, as well as relationships among Jesus' followers, distinctive.

Reflection

- Meditate further on Jesus' need to know that he was loved and chosen by the Father, and how that knowledge enabled him to serve others humbly in love.
- What do you personally learn from the way in which Jesus washed the feet of his disciples?

4
Servants one and all

An example is given not to be admired but to be followed. Jesus has modelled for us true servanthood and, because a servant is not greater than his master, we who are called to follow in his steps will naturally be drawn to a life of service. Jesus concluded his teaching on washing one another's feet with a promise: 'Now that you know these things, you will be blessed if you do them' (John 13:17). The portrait of Christ given in the first Servant Song therefore becomes a continuing pattern for those who are his disciples.

The metaphor of servanthood is, without doubt, at the heart of the Christian life. Indeed, conversion can be viewed as an exchange of masters, from sin to righteousness, and from self to God: 'But now that you have been set free from sin and have become slaves to God, the benefit you reap leads to holiness, and the result is eternal life' (Romans 6:22). Coming to faith in Christ involves a major shift in allegiance and in who is in control of our lives. Describing the whole-hearted response of the Thessalonians to the gospel, Paul sums it up like this: 'You turned to God from idols to serve the living and true God' (1 Thessalonians 1:9). Such a turnaround is life-changing for it involves not just the external relinquishment of idolatry (and every kind of false god, including self) but also an internal acceptance of the rule of God in the whole of life.

The main word for 'servant' in the New Testament is *doulos*, a Greek word meaning 'bond-servant'. In the Roman world of the first century, where slavery was common, a bond-servant was someone who belonged to his master and served not for wages but out of necessity. Such slaves were generally treated well and carried great responsibility in rural estates, commercial enterprises and domestic settings, but they were not free to follow their own will; they were obligated to do their master's bidding.

When we think about being a servant in the biblical sense, the obligation is a spiritual one. We are not forced to serve God but choose to do so, and two illustrations help us to understand this idea of serving willingly.

Slavery was permitted In the Old Testament but only under certain strict guidelines. One was that after serving for six years, a slave had to be released and sent away with generous provision to start a new life. However, the slave could choose, out of love for his master, to stay and be a servant for life—what we might call a 'love-slave' (see Deuteronomy 15:12–17). It is this kind of devotion that is behind the idea of service to God. We serve because we love God.

A similar thought occurs in the New Testament picture of redemption, a metaphor taken from the slave market. To be redeemed was to be set free from slavery through the payment of a price. The idea is that a wealthy person purchases a slave at auction but then, in kindness, chooses to give the slave his freedom. However, out of gratitude, the slave chooses to serve his new master and be bonded to him, albeit as a free man and becoming what we might call a 'free-slave'. This imagery is behind Jesus' use of the word 'ransom' in Mark 10:45 and Paul's teaching about having been bought with a price (1 Corinthians 6:20; 7:22–23). We serve because we are grateful for our salvation.

Several of the New Testament writers used the self-designation 'servant [*doulos*] of God' without any hesitation, reflecting the fact that they were living their lives for the glory of God and seeking to do his will. Not only Paul does this, but also James, Peter, Jude and John (Titus 1:1; James 1:1; 2 Peter 1:1; Jude 1; Revelation 1:1). Nor is such a designation reserved for some band of super-elite believers. All God's people are called to serve him with equal abandonment: 'Never be lacking in zeal, but keep your spiritual fervour, serving the Lord' (Romans 12:11). What is more, serving God is not to be confined to church matters. We serve God wherever we are and in whatever we do. Paul counsels those who are still serving earthly masters to do so as if they are serving the Lord: 'Obey them not only to win their favour when their eye is on you, but like slaves of Christ, doing the will of God from your heart. Serve wholeheartedly, as if you were serving the Lord, not men' (Ephesians 6:6–7). Then, to abolish for all time the false dichotomy between sacred and secular occupations, and to bring all our working lives into the spiritual, he says, 'It is the Lord Christ you are serving' (Colossians 3:24).

This thought leads us naturally to consider the second word for 'servant' in the New Testament, *diakonos*, which refers more to the activity of serving and to what the servant actually does. It reminds us that, because we are servants of God, we will express our devotion to him in the joyful service of those around us. John Finney puts the two words together like this: 'If *doulos* primarily emphasises the relation of the servant to his master, *diakonos* emphasises the relation to his people: *doulos* is vertical, *diakonos* is horizontal.'[1]

Paul was quite clear that his job—and that of all who are gifted in leadership—was not to do the work of ministry on behalf of others but to equip them so that they too could be involved in ministry: 'It was he who gave some to be apostles, some to be prophets, some to be evangelists, and some to be pastors and teachers, *to prepare God's people for works of service*, so that the body of Christ may be built up' (Ephesians 4:11–12, my italics). It is one of the great weaknesses of today's church that, often, we have not followed this principle but have placed a stranglehold on ministry by creating a clergy–laity distinction in some cases and a 'full-time' ministry category in others. All of God's people are called to serve him and to see themselves as God's servants. Only when the whole body of Christ is released in this way will the church be able to fulfil its calling effectively.

Within a local congregation, there are many opportunities for the expression of servanthood, and Christian communities should be characterised by a humble, Christ-like serving of one another. Paul's watchword is simple and direct: 'Serve one another in love'

(Galatians 5:13). This means that we gladly make our gifts, talents and resources available to others. Peter says, 'Each one should use whatever gift he has received to serve others, faithfully administering God's grace in its various forms' (1 Peter 4:10), reminding us that we are only stewards of what has first been entrusted to us by God. So we serve our brothers and sisters by exercising our gifts of preaching, teaching, hospitality, giving and so on for their benefit. We do not hold such gifts as if they were our private possession but readily use them for the good of the body as and when required, even at personal cost.

Richard Foster includes service among the nine spiritual disciplines that he explores in *Celebration of Discipline*. He rightly makes a distinction between choosing to serve and choosing to be a servant. 'When we choose to serve,' he says, 'we are still in charge. We decide whom we will serve and when we will serve… But when we choose to be a servant we give up the right to be in charge. There is great freedom in this.'[2] This reminds us that service is not so much about specific acts as about an attitude of heart and an approach to life, and also that practising the discipline of service (that is, consciously looking for ways to express genuine servanthood) is one of the best ways to grow in humility: true service brings us into the realm of the hidden, the mundane and the ordinary and keeps our feet on the ground.

Servanthood, in the way we are thinking about it, is not restricted within the walls of the church or even within the network of believers. It flows out into our communities and into all the world, for service is the lifeblood of the body of Christ. Those who have servanthood in their hearts will automatically reach out to people in need and will find practical ways of bringing the love of Christ into their neighbourhoods and the troubled places of the world. Likewise, those who see themselves first and foremost as servants of God will do whatever job they have been called to do with a servant heart. Whether in teaching, health care, social work, business, civil service or anywhere else, they will operate from a spirit of self-giving love and a humble desire to help others.

How, though, do we develop such an attitude? Is it that we try to imitate Jesus, copying his ways and living by a moral code of selflessness? We could try that, and we may succeed for a while, but servanthood can never be sustained if it is merely external. No, it has to come from within. It is a matter of the heart.

Jesus took the form of a servant because servanthood is part of his very nature. When we come to faith in Christ, not only are our sins forgiven but we are joined to him in a spiritual union whereby we share his life. We are joined to him as a branch is joined to a vine, and his life begins to flow into us (John 15:1–8). Since he is by nature a servant, we begin to share his love of serving, and the more we abide in him, the more his servant heart is formed within us. This has to be our starting point.

Next, if we truly desire to become servants of God, we will almost certainly be called upon to walk our own version of the downward way that Jesus walked, as described in Philippians 2:5–11, and this will be a continuing process. There may well be some things that we are asked to let go of, such as status and position, cherished ambitions or personal goals, even important relationships and things we considered our 'rights'. Perhaps we will be called to 'empty' ourselves in some specific ways, choosing hiddenness over being well-known, living simply instead of extravagantly, giving ourselves to others rather than climbing the ladder of success. Almost certainly we will be taught the lessons of humility, submission and costly obedience, and we will learn (probably with tears) what it means to deny ourselves and suffer for Christ. Only when we have reached the bottom, as it were, will we be ready to handle the power and authority that come with spiritual servanthood.

Even as this inward work is developing, there will be the daily God-given opportunities for us to take up the towel of service and get our hands wet in the business of foot-washing—that is, practically helping other people. Situations will arise that require us to lay aside our own concerns for a while in order to meet the needs of others. We will need to exercise patience, forbearance, understanding, tolerance, forgiveness and grace in great measure and, often, to receive such blessings for ourselves as we become vulnerable and authentic. We will need to be disciplined to do things we don't want to do, resilient to cope with setbacks and disappointments, and willing to do whatever is asked of us. And always, because we are operating out of the life of Christ, his divine life will be welling up within us, causing our service to be expressed in joy and motivated by love.

The servant metaphor is not the only picture for the Christian life, however; indeed, it is not the most important one. Jesus said to his disciples, 'I no longer call you servants, because a servant does not know his master's business. Instead, I have called you friends, because everything that I learned from my Father I have made known to you' (John 15:14–15). In saying this, he was not dismissing servanthood but explaining how it can be maintained—by developing an intimate relationship with him, abiding in him as a branch abides in the vine.

The great danger in emphasising servanthood is that we move into overdrive, doing as much as we can to show how effective we are and, in our busyness, losing the closeness of our relationship with Christ, on which it all depends. We can become detached from the vine and end up as a withered branch (John 15:6), working for Christ but having no time to be with him. Christ has set his love upon us and delights in us just as he was the object of the Father's love; and he has chosen us and appointed us to go and bear much fruit, just as the Father chose and appointed him (vv. 9, 16). These truths should never be separated but held together in creative tension. Intimacy and activity belong together, and a life of fruitful service is the outcome of a life of continual abiding.

Reflection

- Why is it important that servanthood is at the heart of a congregation?
- How do you understand the connection between friendship with Jesus and the role of a servant?

The
Servant's
Calling

5

The Spirit upon him

I will put my Spirit on him.
ISAIAH 42:1

The servant has been chosen by God for a particular task and mission, which he accepts willingly, but, before the nature of his work is explained, he is given the assurance of divine assistance. There are several ways by which the Lord will uphold his servant but, to begin with, he is told that he will receive the help of the Spirit of God.

This is a clear indication that the servant will not be able to carry out his mission in his own strength. Human energy and natural gifting, strength of personality and determination of will are not sufficient. He will have to discover the reality that every servant of God must come to know—that by ourselves we cannot do the work of God. It must be as the prophet Zechariah told the pioneering post-exilic leader Zerubbabel: '"Not by might nor by power, but by my Spirit," says the Lord Almighty' (Zechariah 3:6).

We normally associate the work of the Holy Spirit with the New Testament period and the days after Pentecost, but, while it is true that the Spirit's activity is much fuller under the new covenant, he is far from absent in the Old Testament era. We often read how the Spirit 'came upon' designated individuals to enable them to fulfil their calling, as, for instance, during the period of the judges (Judges 3:10; 6:34; 11:29; 14:6, 19; 15:14). It was recognised that kings and prophets could not operate apart from the gift of the Spirit, and so they were anointed for their office as a recognition that they were being set apart by God and endued with his Spirit (1 Samuel 9:16; 16:12–13; 1 Kings 1:34; 19:16). It seems that Isaiah himself was aware of the work of the Holy Spirit in his calling to be a prophet: 'And now the Sovereign Lord has sent me, with his Spirit' (48:16). He shared with other prophets, too, a clear expectation of a future day when the Spirit of God would be released into all the earth (Isaiah 32:15; 44:3; Joel 2:28).

With this background, it is not surprising that the servant is linked to the Holy Spirit. The expression 'put my Spirit on him' suggests a deliberate and purposeful act of God, leading to a permanent enduement. This is not to be an ecstatic moment that quickly passes but an ongoing enabling so that the servant will be characterised throughout his ministry by the presence and power of the Spirit. It is hard, therefore, not to associate the servant with two other passages in Isaiah where the Spirit is given to a chosen individual.

The first appears to speak about a future ancestor of King David ('a shoot from the stump of Jesse') whose life is characterised by the Spirit: 'The Spirit of the Lord will rest on him—the Spirit of wisdom and understanding, the Spirit of counsel and of power, the Spirit of knowledge and of the fear of the Lord—and he will delight in the fear of the Lord' (Isaiah 11:2–3).

The second speaks about an individual who is aware of the Spirit's presence and enabling in his ministry: 'The Spirit of the Sovereign Lord is on me, because the Lord has anointed me to preach good news to the poor. He has sent me to bind up the brokenhearted, to proclaim freedom for the captives and release from darkness for the prisoners' (Isaiah 61:1).

Once this connection is made, it is natural then to see an identification between the servant and the promised Messiah, or Anointed One (Psalm 2:2). They are one and the same person, and both find their fulfilment in the person of Jesus, to whom the ascription 'Christ' (Greek for 'anointed one') is readily given in the New Testament. He is the one on whom the Spirit rests in full measure (John 3:34).

Before we look specifically at the work of the Spirit in the life of

Jesus, I want to consider the relationship of the Son to the Father as well, because in this passage we see the Trinity in operation—Father, Son and Holy Spirit working together. It is important to state that the members of the Trinity are equal in their status. Father, Son and Spirit are all equally God and one in essence. However, there does appear to be distinctions between them when it comes to their roles or functions, which can be expressed simply like this: what the Father plans the Son effects, and what the Son effects the Spirit applies. Thus they work together in mutual submission. There is no jockeying for position, no competing for glory, no envy of another's role. Each operates as a servant to the others, and they work in perfect harmony and without discord. Thus the Trinity presents us with a model for all human relationships, based on humility, not hierarchy; servanthood and mutual submission, not pride and selfish ambition—and the model includes church leadership, marriage and family life, teamwork in organisations and so on.

We see this harmony beautifully displayed in the work of salvation. It is the Father who plans for it and sends the Son as the servant; it is the Son who willingly comes and lays down his life; and it is the Spirit who convicts us of our sin and points us to the Saviour, thus applying the finished work of the Son to human lives and bringing glory to the Father.

I want to draw your attention to something that is often called the 'subordination' of the Son, and how he willingly places himself under the authority of the Father, submitting his will to the Father's. Here we see a divine humility that was at work even before the incarnation took place. The Son was already a servant in heaven. It was inevitable that, when he became man, it would be in the form of a servant: he could be no other.

What this does is to highlight the beauty of subordination and submission. We tend to shy away from such concepts because they can be abused, but true servanthood is impossible without them. When the humble model of the Trinity is followed and we see ourselves primarily as servants of others, there will be no exploitation or domineering, only a looking after the best interests of others. We begin from a place of submission to Christ, and then of mutual submission to one another. This applies to each of us. As Richard Foster notes concerning the discipline of submission:

It is a posture obligatory upon all Christians; men as well as women, fathers as well as children, masters as well as slaves. We are commanded to live a life of submission because Jesus lived a life of submission, not because we are in a particular place or station in life. Self-denial is a posture fitting those who follow a crucified Lord.[3]

Jesus lived his life in submission to the Father and, what is more, in dependency upon the Holy Spirit. Here is another amazing aspect of his humility. Having become a real man, he had to live his earthly life as we do, out of his humanity, and thus he too required the help of the Spirit. The coming of the Spirit upon him at his baptism was not a publicity stunt or empty showpiece; it was a necessary event, identifying him as the servant but also empowering him for his task.

Luke seems to have had a particular interest in the work of the Spirit, both in his Gospel and in his recording of the Acts of the Apostles (sometimes alternatively named the Acts of the Holy Spirit). He highlights the work of the Spirit towards Jesus, especially in the early days of his ministry, and we can see three significant things that the Spirit did for Jesus.

- He confirmed to Jesus his identity as the Son, as one loved by God, and as one with whom God was pleased (Luke 3:21–23). A clear sense of our spiritual identity and calling is essential to fruitful ministry, and knowing that we are loved by God is the only way we can find the resources to serve and love other people. When we know God's approval, we can accept ourselves more easily, and this frees us to accept other people.
- He strengthened Jesus through a time of testing and temptation. Surprisingly, Luke tells us that it was the Spirit who led Jesus

into the wilderness to be tempted by the devil (Luke 4:1–2). Clarity and conviction in our calling, strength of character and the development of inner resolve are not things we are born with. They are formed within us through testing, trial and temptation, and such challenge (courtesy of the Spirit) was necessary for Jesus as well (see Hebrews 2:17–18; 4:15–16; 5:8–9. It will also be the furnace through which the Spirit purifies each one of us.

- He empowered him for his ministry. Jesus returned from his skirmish with the devil, not weakened but strengthened (Luke 4:14) and with a heightened understanding of his mission. In the synagogue at Nazareth, he opened the scripture to the passage in Isaiah 61 that we have already considered, knowing that it was to be fulfilled through him. He could say with conviction, 'The Spirit of the Lord is on me, because he has anointed me' (Luke 4:18). We also can look to the Spirit for his empowerment in our own service.

The Holy Spirit continued to play a significant part in the ministry of Jesus, leading and guiding him, revealing the Father's will to him, showing him things he would not otherwise have known, giving him authority over demons and causing joy to well up within him (for example, John 4:17–19; Matthew 12:28; Luke 10:21). Peter sums up the whole life and ministry of Jesus as being influenced by the Spirit: 'You know... how God anointed Jesus of Nazareth with the Holy Spirit and power, and how he went around doing good and healing all who were under the power of the devil, because God was with him' (Acts 10:37–38). If Jesus needed the help and enabling of the Spirit, how much more do we?

Jesus was concerned that his followers should also have the Spirit after he had left them to return to heaven. He promised them 'another Counsellor' who would not only be with them but would be in them (John 14:16–18, 26; 15:26; 16:7–15). Symbolically he breathed on them as a sign that they would receive the Spirit (20:22). He told them to wait in Jerusalem until they were clothed with power from on high (Luke 24:49) and then, just prior to his ascension, promised them that they would be baptised with the Spirit (Acts 1:5), which would be the empowering they needed to be his witnesses (v. 8). Having ascended to the Father's right hand, he poured out the Spirit upon them on the day of Pentecost (2:33).

It is in this sense that all believers are 'pentecostal', for, since that day, the Spirit has been given to all God's people. He lives within us and our bodies have become his temple (Romans 8:9; 1 Corinthians 3:16; Galatians 4:6). He is the one who equips us by gifting us for ministry (1 Corinthians 12:7–11) and transforms us by helping us to overcome the downward pull of the flesh (the sinful tendency still inherent within each of us) and to produce the fruit of the Spirit in our lives—the characteristics of the life of Christ (see Galatians 5:16–26).

Our responsibility is to submit ourselves to Christ and allow the Holy Spirit to direct us, responding to his leading with faith and obedience. This is described by Paul as being 'filled with the Spirit' (Ephesians 5:18) and seems to be what we might call the 'normal' Christian life—a life lived in dependency on the Spirit where we are daily enabled, equipped and empowered by God. This is the only way by which Christian service, however it is expressed, can be sustained and effective. It is imperative, therefore, that every believer follows the example of Jesus and lives in step with the Spirit.

I grew up as a young believer in the 1960s and '70s, when we experienced in Britain what became known as 'charismatic renewal'. Believers like me who had largely ignored the Holy Spirit and been ignorant of his workings suddenly discovered that there was a third person to the Trinity. Churches that had been staid and conservative were turned upside down as they were released into praise and worship, spiritual gifts, praying for the sick and boldness in witnessing. There were excesses, of course, and an awful lot of pride, so, sadly, the move of God's Spirit became divisive and there was much hurt. I'm glad to say that things have settled down and today there is a much more mature approach to the work of the Spirit. Many of the things that once we fought over are now generally accepted. Those of us who were carried along in the renewal movement are more contrite and humble, and those who opposed it are less defensive and resistant. There is a greater openness all round to the ministry of the Spirit, which is vital if the church is to make an impact in the 21st century.

The need of the hour remains, however, to be filled with the Spirit on a daily basis. It is not my concern to try to influence your theology but to challenge your heart. Each of us must ask the question, 'Am I serving in dependency upon the Holy Spirit?' and must not be satisfied until we know that the Spirit is with us, in us and upon us. It was never God's intention that the servant should struggle to perform the task that God had given him through his own resources, but rather to supply him with everything he would need to be effective. That applies to us, too. God will give us all we need: 'If you then, though you are evil, know how to give good gifts to your children, how much more will your Father in heaven give the Holy Spirit to those who ask him!' (Luke 11:13).

Reflection

- Continue to think about the relationships within the Trinity and, in particular, about the subordination of the Son.
- Spend some time reflecting on your relationship with the Holy Spirit.

6

Justice, the suffering servant and the law of God

I will put my Spirit on him, and he will bring justice to the nations.
ISAIAH 42:1

The Spirit has been given to the Servant so that he is both equipped and empowered for his task. Like all servants, he lives to do the will of another—in this case, the will of God. He has been given a particular assignment, which is summed up in the expression 'bring justice', and the field of his operation is 'to the nations'. The Spirit will enable him to fulfil his calling, which will have an impact far beyond Israel's borders.

'Justice' would not have been the first word that came into my mind, had I been asked to anticipate the ministry of the servant, but that is the word given in scripture. It is not, of course, a strange word to use. We know that God is a God of justice. According to the psalmists, God not only loves justice (Psalm 11:7) but is known for it (9:7–10), and it is the foundation of his rule (89:14). This means that he is worthy of trust: 'He is the Rock, his works are perfect, and all his ways are just. A faithful God who does no wrong, upright and just is he' (Deuteronomy 32:4). Not surprisingly, he wants justice to be seen on the earth, and the servant's ministry will be to bring this about.

As I ponder the calling given to the servant, it seems to me that there are two aspects to the bringing of justice to the nations. The first is with reference to the law of God—the tangible expression of his justice, crystallised in the Ten Commandments—which showed Israel how to live in relationship with God. The second has to do with the outworking of genuine faith and the implication that justice must be seen to be done in the way God's people live, how they treat others and how they respond to the needs of the world—the social dimension of true religion that was also in the law and became a major theme of the prophets. These two aspects of justice represent the twin themes of loving God and loving our neighbour, which are the summary of the law (Matthew 22:37–39).

We will begin by looking at how the servant will bring justice with reference to the law of God. The law was given not as something distinct from God but as an expression of his nature. It expresses what he is like, and the person who keeps the law is therefore considered righteous or godly, and pleasing to God. Because God is just, his law is just, and it was intended not to be a burden but a blessing—the foundation for wise living and a just society. Nehemiah, in restoring the law to Israel after the exile, reminded them of its origin: 'You came down on Mount Sinai; you spoke to them from heaven. You gave them regulations and laws that are just and right, and decrees and commands that are good' (Nehemiah 9:13).

The only problem with the law is that it is impossible to keep it perfectly (as Israel knew too well). When inevitably we break the law, it condemns us, pointing out our failure and passing sentence upon us. That is why sin can be defined as 'transgression', the breaking of the law, or 'trespass', the doing of that which the law forbids. Sin has many consequences. First, it brings pain and misery and broken relationships; life no longer works. Second, it separates us from God, breaking our fellowship with him; he is holy and can have nothing to do with sin. Third, it places us under the wrath of God and the just penalty that sin deserves: 'the wages of sin is death' (Romans 6:23).

God is not only holy, however; he is also merciful and gracious, and this situation created a dilemma for him. How could he uphold the law (which was right and good) and be in relationship with his people (who had sinned and broken the law)? Through the sacrificial system, God made it possible for sinful men and women to be forgiven and return to him. By the offering of a spotless lamb or goat, they could make atonement for their sin and be brought back into fellowship with God. In addition, once a year, atonement was made by the high priest for the whole nation of Israel (Leviticus 16).

It seems that it was never God's intention for the sacrificial system to be permanent. It was designed as a temporary measure until the time was right for something more lasting. Certainly this is how the book of Hebrews 9 and 10 portray it, reminding us that the sacrifices had to be repeated annually (an indication of their temporary nature), and that they did not actually cleanse the conscience of the worshippers (showing their limited effectiveness). A better sacrifice was needed, and this is where the servant (and, of course, Jesus) comes in.

There are indications in the other Servant Songs that the servant will be a suffering servant. We are told that he will be despised and abhorred (Isaiah 49:7) and that he will be beaten and ill-treated (50:6), but it is in the fourth song (52:13—53:12) that we are presented with an amazing prophetic insight into how he will satisfy the law's just demands. It will be through the offering of himself as a living sacrifice, dying as a substitute for guilty sinners. This will be God's way of providing a permanent solution to the problem of human sinfulness, upholding the law and yet being able freely to offer forgiveness and acceptance.

It is impossible to read Isaiah 53 and not think of Jesus, for the events of his death and the meaning given to it are fulfilled with startling accuracy. Theologian Henri Blocher writes:

We believe not only that Jesus is the Servant (that is, that Jesus fulfils what is written of the Servant—a retrospective *interpretation of the prophecy), but also that the Servant is Jesus, and him crucified (that is to say that Isaiah, from his own vantage point in history, looked forward to the coming of Jesus and actually* spoke about him).[4]

It is not my intention to give a detailed interpretation of Isaiah 53, but to draw out the salient points that enable us to see how the servant will bring justice.

What is strikingly obvious is that the servant's ministry will be accomplished through his own death. He is described as 'a man of sorrows, and familiar with suffering' (53:3), someone who has experienced being despised and rejected. Beyond psychological pain, he suffers, at the hands of others, a violent and agonising death. Notice the words that are used: 'stricken', 'smitten', 'pierced' and 'crushed' (vv. 4–5). He is found guilty and taken away to die, even though he has done nothing wrong (vv. 8–9). He moves towards his fate with quiet resignation, like a lamb going to be sacrificed (v.7).

Isaiah describes not only the manner of his death but also its meaning. Surprisingly, it has to do with the will of God (v.10). God allows the servant to suffer because his death is on behalf of others. He is not dying, as some people initially supposed, for his own wrongdoing. God is laying the iniquity of us all on him, and he is taking the punishment in our place, as a substitute (vv. 4–6). In this he has become a 'guilt offering' for the sins of the whole world (v. 10), thus fulfilling the will of God. Blocher summarisees it like this: 'The Servant "makes *himself* an offering for sin"; he offers not another life, but his own as a sin offering. Since he offers the sacrifice, he is the priest; since he offers himself, he is the sacrifice. He himself is the Lamb of God.'[5]

The outcome of this vicarious death is significant, providing a new and permanent way of becoming right with God. The first effect of his death is to 'justify many' (v. 11)—that is, to put them right as far as the law is concerned, now that their sin has been punished. The second effect is to bring healing and peace to those who previously had been riddled with the disease of sin and afflicted with a guilty conscience. How will this come about? As people come to a knowledge of him (v. 11), implying a relationship of love and faith and obedience. Such an achievement is worthy of note, and the servant will be given 'a portion among the great' (v. 12), being raised and lifted up and highly exalted (52:13)— words that imply a subsequent resurrection.

We may wonder whether or not Jesus understood his mission in terms of being the suffering servant. It seems that his awareness of his calling was a gradual one, but, from the time of his baptism, he appears to have known that it would culminate in his death. John the Baptist proclaimed twice in his hearing, 'Look, the Lamb of God!' and, on the first occasion, added '… who takes away the sin of the world' (John 1:29, 36). Jesus seems to have lived with an acute sense of destiny, aware that his 'time' was being apportioned according to a divine timetable and leading up to his 'hour', by which he meant his death (John 2:4; 7:6, 30, 12:27; 17:1).

Several times he spoke openly about what would happen to him. As the good shepherd, he would 'lay down his life' for his sheep— a vicarious act that he would do voluntarily and without coercion (John 10:11–18). This thought is repeated when he tells his disciples in the upper room, 'Greater love has no one than this, that he lay down his life for his friends' (15:13). On another occasion he spoke about being 'lifted up from the earth', signifying that he knew he would die by crucifixion (John 12:32–33). Somewhat unwittingly, the high priest of the day, Caiaphas, 'prophesied' that Jesus would die for the Jewish nation: 'It is better for you that one man die for the people than that the whole nation perish' (John 11:50–51), giving a hint of the substitutionary nature of his death.

The watershed in Jesus' ministry seems to be the moment at Caesarea Philippi when Peter recognised him to be the Son of God (Matthew 16:16), and from that point onwards he speaks often about his forthcoming death, with increasing clarity. There is an inevitability about it, not just because of the growing opposition but because this is where his mission will take him. It will happen in Jerusalem, at the hands of the religious leaders. He will be betrayed and suffer many things before being crucified, but after three days will come back to life (Matthew 16:21). Only once does Jesus seek to interpret his death, when he speaks of it as a 'ransom for many' (Mark 10:45). We have already thought about the metaphor behind this expression, but what is important here is the connection with Isaiah 53 and a substitutionary death that benefits many others. He offers up his life as an act of service, having come not to be served but to serve. Surely he has in mind the suffering servant!

The connection between Jesus and the suffering servant is made even more specific during the last supper. He links the broken bread with his broken body, and the cup he connects with the shedding of his blood, of which he says: 'This is my blood of the covenant, which is poured out for many for the forgiveness of sins' (Matthew 26:28). We cannot fail to see echoes of Isaiah 53 in the language used—a death that is because of sin, that benefits many and brings forgiveness and a new way of relating to God. Just as the servant 'makes his life a guilt offering' (Isaiah 53:10), so Jesus offers his life as a sacrifice for sin.

It is Paul, however, who makes explicit the connection between the death of Jesus and the law of God. The idea of 'justification' is only one of several ways of understanding the death of Christ, but, for Paul, it is perhaps the most significant. The metaphor is taken from the law court and has to do with acquittal from the law's just condemnation of sin. Just as, in a court of law, a person may be declared acquitted, which means they are free from the law's demands, so Paul believes that a person is declared righteous before God because Jesus, as the person's representative or sub-stitute, took the punishment for sin that was due to them. The law's demands have been satisfied and they are now free. A divine exchange has taken place: 'God made him who had no sin to be sin for us, so that in him we might become the righteousness of God' (2 Corinthians 5:21).

The immediate benefit of Christ's death is that we are forgiven and have peace with God (Romans 5:1). We are considered 'justi-fied' because the law has been satisfied, and this status becomes ours when we believe in Jesus. Faith involves a personal trusting of ourselves to God's way of salvation in Christ and a giving up of any attempt to justify ourselves by our own endeavours. Justification is a gift of grace, received by faith. Paul makes two major statements that capture the heart of this:

This righteousness from God comes through faith in Jesus Christ to all who believe. There is no difference, for all have sinned and fall short of the glory of God, and are justified freely by his grace through the redemption that came by Christ Jesus. (Romans 3:22–24)

We who are Jews by birth and not 'Gentile sinners' know that a man is not justified by observing the law, but by faith in Jesus Christ. So we, too, have put our faith in Christ Jesus that we may be justified by faith in Christ and not by observing the law, because by observing the law no one will be justified. (Galatians 2:15–16)

This, then, is God's way of bringing people into a right relationship with himself, and it is good news indeed. Paul gave himself as a servant to preaching the message of the cross and of justification by faith—first to his own people, the Jews, and then, because of their hardness of heart, to the Gentiles. This second movement in mission, to those outside Israel, happened in fulfilment of the second Servant Song and so that justice could come to all the nations. In turning to the Gentiles, Paul was conscious of this very fact: 'For this is what the Lord has commanded us: "I have made you a light for the Gentiles, that you may bring salvation to the ends of the earth"' (Acts 13:47, quoting Isaiah 49:6).

The work of justification is accomplished by God through Christ, and there is nothing we are required to do to bring it about. We do not bring justice to the nations; that is the servant's work, and it has been made possible through the cross of Christ. Our privilege and responsibility is to make this good news known and to proclaim it to the ends of the earth. This is what motivates the work of evangelism (proclamation within our own culture) and mission (proclamation to people of other cultures). We have a message to proclaim and must make it known in every possible way, using all our God-given creativity and ingenuity.

The medium of communication will change and vary depending on the culture and the context, but the message stays the same and, at its heart, is very simple. As Paul says, 'For what I received I passed on to you as of first importance: that Christ died for our sins according to the Scriptures, that he was buried, that he was raised on the third day' (1 Corinthians 15:3–4). It is wonderful to see new expressions of church springing up in many parts of the world as God's people continue their servant task of communicating the message in relevant and accessible ways to a fast-changing world. However, in the need to be 'up to date' and with the freedom to experiment, we must never decentralise this fundamental truth. The message of the cross must always be paramount.

Preaching and teaching, in their various formats, will continue to be part of our communication strategy. According to Isaiah, it is in the servant's teaching that the islands will put their hope (Isaiah 42:4), so proclaiming the message of Christ has a high priority. It is our privilege to be able to share the good news, and for this great task we too need the help and enabling of the Spirit. As John Stott reminds us, 'The preacher is a divine agent or *diakonos*, and all his service will be lost if God does not powerfully work through him to create faith in the hearers of the Word.'[6]

Reflection

- Ponder some more about the portrait of Jesus as the suffering servant and what he has done for you.
- In what ways are you able to proclaim the message of the cross? Pray that you will be used by God to share this wonderful good news.

7

Justice, the compassionate servant and the needs of the world

In faithfulness he will bring forth justice; he will not falter or be discouraged till he establishes justice on earth.

ISAIAH 42:3–4

The first part of the servant's mission is to satisfy the demands of God's broken law and to bring justice by offering himself as a sacrifice for the sin of the world. In this way, God is seen to be just and yet also able to justify guilty sinners (Romans 3:26). This, however, is only half the equation. The second part of his mission is to confront the injustice that exists within society, showing that God cares and will respond.

Isaiah himself knew only too well that God was concerned about the plight of the poor and needy. He found himself, as many of the prophets did, speaking out in God's name against the injustices of his own society and the falsity of religious behaviour devoid of a social conscience:

When you spread out your hands in prayer, I will hide my eyes from you; even if you offer many prayers, I will not listen. Your hands are full of blood; wash and make yourselves clean. Take your evil deeds out of my sight! Stop doing wrong, learn to do right! Seek justice, encourage the oppressed. Defend the cause of the fatherless, plead the case of the widow. (Isaiah 1:15–17)

For Isaiah, true religion was not about religious practices so much as about compassionate action to help those in need:

'Is not this the kind of fasting I have chosen: to loose the chains of injustice and untie the cords of the yoke, to set the oppressed free and break every yoke? Is it not to share your food with the hungry and to provide the poor wanderer with shelter—when you see the naked, to clothe him, and not to turn away from your own flesh and blood?' (58:6–7)

He considered that serving the poor was not only the right thing to do, but the best way to bring God's blessing to the nation.

Other prophets shared a similar perspective. Amos, the farmer turned prophet, declared, 'Away with the noise of your songs! I will not listen to the music of your harps. But let justice roll on like a river, righteousness like a never-failing stream' (Amos 5:23–24). Micah was equally forthright: 'He has showed you, O man, what is good. And what does the Lord require of you? To act justly and to love mercy and to walk humbly with your God' (Micah 6:8). Jeremiah contrasts godly king Josiah's compassion with the greed of his wayward son Shallum:

'He did what was right and just, so all went well with him. He defended the cause of the poor and needy, and so all went. Is that not what it means to know me?' declares the Lord. 'But your eyes and your heart are set only on dishonest gain, on shedding innocent blood and on oppression and extortion.' (Jeremiah 22:16–17)

Given the concern of God for the poor, it is inconceivable that the servant could be anything but interested in their welfare and in correcting the ills of society. Those who have no voice need someone to speak out for them; those who are powerless need someone to champion their cause, and those who are without hope need someone to come to their aid.

This great concern must have been in the mind of Jesus as he entered the synagogue at Nazareth at the beginning of his public ministry. With all eyes fixed upon him, the passage he chose to read was a declaration of intent, a statement of his mission: 'The Spirit of the Lord is on me, because he has anointed me to preach good news to the poor. He has sent me to proclaim freedom for the prisoners and recovery of sight for the blind, to release the oppressed, to proclaim the year of the Lord's favour' (Luke 4:18–19; see Isaiah 61:1–2).

Yes, he had come to bring good news to those who were spiritually poor, bound by sin, blinded by Satan and oppressed by demonic forces, but Jesus was not simply speaking figuratively; he meant it literally. He came to inaugurate a new kingdom that was based on justice and a compassion for the poor and needy. He travelled extensively, preaching the good news of the kingdom, aware that this was his calling (Luke 4:43; Matthew 9:35–36). He summed up his own ministry like this: 'The blind receive sight, the lame walk, those who have leprosy are cured, the deaf hear, the dead are raised, and the good news is preached to the poor' (Matthew 11:5). This was how he lived himself and how he wanted his disciples to live also.

Jesus was a man filled with compassion. The Gospels describe the emotion that Jesus felt when he saw need, either in the crowds or in individual sufferers, in a way that seems unusual to us. They use the Greek word *splanknon*, which means 'to be moved in one's bowels', to be stirred deeply within and moved not just to pity but to action. This was how Jesus reacted when he encountered a leper, met the widow in Nain whose son had died, saw the lostness of the multitudes, felt the pain of the sick, heard the cry of the beggars and responded to the plight of a broken-hearted father (Mark 1:41; 9:22; Matthew 14:14; 15:32; Luke 7:13). There was within him an instinctive and generous-hearted responsiveness to the needs of humanity. He could not remain aloof or detached; nor could he turn a blind eye and become indifferent. He was compelled by love to do something.

Jesus taught his followers the importance of giving to the poor (Matthew 19:21, Luke 12:33) and the joy of being welcoming and hospitable towards those who are less fortunate (Luke 14:12–14).

He rebuked the Pharisees because they neglected justice and the love of God (Luke 11:42). He summed up the law in two challenging statements: love God, and love your neighbour (10:27–28), and illustrated what it means to be a neighbour, through the parable of the good Samaritan (vv. 30–37). The Samaritan 'took pity' (*splanknon*) on the man who had been attacked, tending to his wounds, taking him to a place of refuge and paying for his care. A true neighbour is one who shows mercy to others, regardless of nationality, and Jesus encouraged his listeners to 'go and do likewise' (v. 37).

Perhaps the parable of the sheep and the goats in Matthew 25:31–46 best sums up what Jesus wanted to teach his followers. The sheep (who inherit the kingdom) are those who have fed the hungry, helped the thirsty, welcomed the stranger, clothed the beggar, cared for the sick and visited people in prison. The goats by contrast (who do not inherit the kingdom) are those who have not done these things. The sheep have acted unselfconsciously and not for reward, because they have done it for 'the very least', those who could never repay them. Yet in serving the least fortunate they have actually been serving Christ, for he has identified himself with the poor. It was this amazing truth that motivated Mother Teresa and her Sisters of Charity in their care of the poor and dying in Calcutta. She said, 'Jesus makes himself the hungry one, the naked one, the homeless one, the sick one, the one in prison, the lonely one, the unwanted one, and he says, "You did it to me". He is hungry for our love, and this is the hunger of our poor people.'[7]

It should be clear from all this that those who have been justified by faith will express that faith through their involvement in the issues of social justice. Grace should make us just. This has not always been the case: for some evangelical Christians, the fear of losing the message of the cross in a plethora of social action has meant they have shied away from such involvement. Gradually, however, over the last 30 years or so, they have come to realise that the proclamation of the gospel and the demonstration of the love of God belong together. A turning point was the Lausanne

Congress of 1974, and one of the main architects was John Stott. Stott believed that there should be a synthesis between evangelism and social action, and that this was possible in the servant role. 'If we truly love our neighbour we shall without doubt tell him the Good News of Jesus,' he said. 'But equally if we truly love our neighbour we won't stop there... Love... expresses itself in service wherever it sees need.'[8]

The needs of the world have never been greater than they are today. The poor and needy, the marginalised and victimised, the abused and exploited, the deprived and neglected, the hungry and the thirsty still cry out for help. The plight of women and children, of refugees and displaced people, of the illiterate and the homeless, of orphans and widows, of AIDS sufferers and the victims of war, does not go away or decrease. Millions are trapped within social, political, cultural and economic systems that imprison them in poverty, sickness and despair. They are oppressed and powerless. Are we aware of their need? Do we care enough to get involved? How should a servant respond? The great injustice of the 21st century is that so much of this suffering is unnecessary. We have the resources and technology to make a difference, if we have the will-power.

One writer has expressed the challenge we face like this:

There is much at stake. The world we live in is under siege—three billion are desperately poor, one billion hungry, millions are trafficked in human slavery, ten million children die needlessly each year, wars and conflicts are wreaking havoc, pandemic diseases are spreading, ethnic hatred is flaming, and terrorism is growing. Most of our brothers and sisters in the developing world live in grinding poverty. And in the midst stands the Church of Jesus Christ... with resources, knowledge, and tools unequalled in the history of Christendom. I believe we stand on the brink of a defining moment. We have a choice to make.[9]

That choice, of course, is whether or not to get involved. Even when we have a servant's heart, we may not always get the point.

Many Christians in the developed world are trapped in affluent lifestyles, living for our careers and following our own dreams of success both for ourselves and our children. We don't want to be inconvenienced, let alone suffer, and we do not take the demands of the gospel seriously. We give as little as we can and are so focused on ourselves that we remain blind to the real issues of the world. If we are honest, we often feel that the poor are poor because they are lazy; that people have AIDS because of their lifestyles; that the sick should take better care of themselves in the first place. We have much to repent of if we are to live out true servanthood.

Yet there are those who give themselves sacrificially to bringing justice to the needy, burying themselves in the broken places of the world in obedience to Jesus. Indeed, for me, it is one of the great affirmations of the truth of Christianity that wherever in the world there is need—because of natural disasters, famines, wars and so on—there you will find God's people, quietly and unobtrusively caring and serving. God is at work through them, meeting the needs of those who suffer, bringing justice to the nations.

Richard Stearns was CEO of an American tableware company with a successful career. Married with five children, he lived in a large house, drove a Jaguar and travelled widely, always first-class and staying in the best hotels. Respected in his community, influential in his large suburban church and generous in his charitable giving, he was the epitome of a 'successful' Christian—or so he thought. Out of the blue he was invited to become President of World Vision, a Christian organisation dedicated to working with families and children and to tacking the causes of poverty and injustice. He felt inadequate and unqualified for such a role and resisted the opportunity until God showed him without any shadow of a doubt that this was the job for him.

The move meant a change of location for his family and a huge drop in salary, but more significant was the impact it made on his faith. His first trip abroad (to Uganda) completely took him apart, showing him at first-hand the suffering of AIDS victims, especially children. Overwhelmed by what he saw, his tears began to flow. He describes the moment like this:

'Forgive me, Lord, forgive me, I didn't know.' But I did know. I knew about poverty and suffering in the world. I was aware that children die daily from starvation and lack of clean water. I also knew about AIDS and the orphans it leaves behind, but I kept these things outside of my insulating bubble and looked the other way. Yet this was to be the moment that would ever after define me… My sadness that day was replaced by repentance. Despite what the Bible had told me so clearly, I had turned a blind eye to the poor.[10]

Stearns recognised that there was a 'hole' in his gospel, a blind spot in his understanding of Christianity. He began to see that being a Christian, a follower of Jesus, requires more than just having a personal and transforming relationship with God. It also entails a public and transforming relationship with the world. If our faith has no positive outward expression, then it has a 'hole' in it. As the apostle James put it, 'faith without deeds is dead' (James 2:26).

Mei Ling (not her real name) was attending a retreat in Malaysia, taking a few days out to listen to God and to mull over her future. A social worker for the Singapore government, she had worked with delinquent girls for more than 13 years but was considering an invitation to go 'full-time' and become Director of a Christian charity that ran a halfway house for women prisoners and drug addicts. Not having had theological training, she felt inadequate for the task, and it would also mean a big pay cut. However, as she pondered the Servant Song in Isaiah 42:1–9, she was struck by the promise of verses 6–7: 'I, the Lord, have called you in righteousness; I will take hold of your hand. I will keep you and will make you to be a covenant for the people and a light for the Gentiles, to open eyes that are blind, to free captives from prison and to release from the dungeon those who sit in darkness.'

That was the confirmation she needed: Mei Ling left the retreat with the assurance that God was calling her to this work and she should step out of her comfort zone.

These stories recount the experiences of just two individuals who have looked at the needs of the world through the eyes of a servant and felt compelled to respond. All of us who take seriously the claims of Christ upon our lives and seek to walk the path of servanthood must consider carefully how we can integrate compassion for the poor into our discipleship. In what way can we be involved in bringing justice to the nations?

It is not easy. I am writing this chapter in the run-up to Christmas. We have stocked up with extra food (the freezer is full), bought our presents (what do you give to someone who has everything?) and are looking forward to 'spoiling' our first grandchild (who, at just a few weeks old, has already been deluged with everything a baby could want). I am resisting the temptation to buy a more up-to-date TV in the January sales (LED or LCD?) and am debating in my mind if I should buy an Amazon Kindle (basic or with keyboard?) or maybe even an iPad (version 1 or 2?). At the same time I am writing about poverty, starvation and child mortality. Hmm… perhaps there is a 'hole' in my gospel, too.

Reflection

- Meditate upon the compassion of Jesus for those in need, thinking of some of the examples given in this chapter.
- 'Grace should make us just' (p. 54). How is this being worked out in your life?

The
Servant's
Character

8

The servant as leader

We begin to focus now on the character of the servant, because the Father's delight is as much in who the servant is as in what the servant does. Of course his work is important but the manner in which he goes about that work is just as pleasing. It is a common tendency to appreciate people for their giftedness, and exceptionally gifted people often rise to prominence despite weaknesses in their character. Scripture, however, asserts the primacy of character over gifting.

We will look at three outstanding aspects of the servant's character that are mentioned in Isaiah 42, but first we will consider the important matter of Christian leadership. Why? Because it is clear that the servant is also a leader. That may sound like a contradiction in terms, because servants do not normally lead. Servants do what leaders tell them, and leaders give instructions to their servants. That is the ordinary way of things. The portrait we have here of the servant, however, changes all that and introduces us to servant-leadership, a distinctly Christian approach to power and authority that was modelled by Jesus and is given as a pattern for his disciples.

What do we mean by servant-leadership? Simply this—that those who lead in God's way do so with humility, recognising that their leadership ability is a gift from him, which they gladly exercise on behalf of others as their way of serving the body. In other words, they serve by leading and they lead by serving. Thus the servant described in Isaiah 42 is humble in his approach to leadership despite the temptation to pride (v. 2), compassionate in his relationship to his followers despite their brokenness (v. 3) and faithful in carrying out his task despite the pain involved (v. 4).

This kind of leadership was exemplified by Jesus. He had a clear vision, fulfilling the mandate of the servant in doing the Father's will. He went out ahead, leading the way in obedience and inviting others to join him, with the words, 'Follow me.' He gathered around him a group of disciples whom he taught and instructed, mentoring them and preparing them for future service, shaping their characters and developing their potential. He was their Teacher and Lord, but never in a domineering way, always acting from humility and looking out for their best interests. All of this was illustrated in his washing of their feet (John 13:1–17).

The disciples had grown up with their own cultural views of leadership. Being Jewish, they would have been influenced by what they saw in their religious leaders, especially the Pharisees, but Jesus warned them against emulating those leaders' example. According to Matthew's Gospel, the Pharisees were particularly addicted to the praise of other people, to making a good impression and to the enjoyment of status and position, but Jesus warned his disciples against all that: 'But you are not to be called "Rabbi", for you have only one Master and you are all brothers. And do not call anyone on earth 'father', for you have one Father, and he is in heaven. Nor are you to be called 'teacher', for you have one Teacher, the Christ' (Matthew 23:8–10). Then he explained his new way: 'The greatest among you will be your servant. For whoever exalts himself will be humbled, and whoever humbles himself will be exalted' (vv. 11–12).

True leadership is exercised with a light touch. Servant leaders respect those whom they lead, seeing them as equals, not subordinates. Their aim is to serve in whatever way they can, not to climb an ecclesiastical ladder or make a name for themselves. They are as content with the background as the limelight, and with hiddenness as prominence, because they are not seeking their own advantage or ambition.

Another influence on the disciples' thinking would have been the Roman occupying army with its hierarchical structure and chain of command, which can be seen in the centurion's response to

Jesus: 'I myself am a man under authority, with soldiers under me. I tell this one, "Go," and he goes; and that one, "Come,", and he comes. I say to my servant, "Do this," and he does it' (Luke 7:8). From this perspective, leadership is about the exercise of power and authority, telling others what to do and issuing commands and instructions. It is a top-down model of leadership, perhaps the most commonly held view of all. Most people imagine leadership as sitting at the top of the pyramid and being in control, so, when they come into leadership, this is how they behave.

Jesus, however, contradicts such an approach; indeed, he turns it upside down:

Jesus called them together and said, 'You know that those who are regarded as rulers of the Gentiles lord it over them, and their high officials exercise authority over them. Not so with you. Instead, whoever wants to become great among you must be your servant, and whoever wants to be first must be slave of all. For even the Son of Man did not come to be served, but to serve, and to give his life as a ransom for many.' (Mark 10:42–45, my emphasis)

Jesus here redefines leadership. It is exactly the opposite of what his disciples have known previously. Leaders may be at the point of the triangle, but the triangle is inverted, illustrating that leaders serve the people they lead by encouraging and equipping them, releasing them into their God-given destinies and enabling them to be effective. They do not use people to meet their own ego-needs for success and achievement or to achieve their personal goals, whether for financial reward or material benefit. They gladly give themselves to the welfare of others, even at personal cost, and refuse to manipulate or pressurise the people they lead. They are always asking, 'How can I help you? How can I promote your growth in God? How can we, together, be more effective for the kingdom?'

It is of interest that, in recent times, servant-leadership has been seen by many secular thinkers as the kind of leadership needed in today's society. One of its main exponents was Robert Greenleaf, a business executive and university lecturer in America. He wrote his seminal work on leadership in 1970, calling it *Servant Leadership*, and his approach has influenced many in their thinking about leadership in the realms of business, education, politics and, of course, religion.

Greenleaf's basic thesis is that leaders must be servants first:

It begins with the natural feeling that one wants to serve, to serve first. Then conscious choice brings one to aspire to lead. That person is sharply different from one who is leader first, perhaps because of the need to assuage an unusual power drive or to acquire material possessions. For such it will be a later choice to serve—after leadership is established. The leader-first and the servant-first are two extreme types.[11]

It seems to me that Greenleaf is saying exactly what Isaiah and Jesus were saying, and that he has put his finger on the key issue: the best leaders are servants at heart, and service, rather than position or power, is their starting point. What an amazing difference there would be if this attitude could be the bottom line for everyone in all churches and Christian organisations—for those who lead and those who follow. Almost certainly, church would be more enjoyable, leaders would be more motivated and the gospel would be more effectively proclaimed. All in leadership should honestly ask themselves the question, 'Do I lead to serve others, or do I lead to serve myself?'

Greenleaf went on to say that we can tell if people are leading as servants by looking at the outcomes of their leadership:

The best test, and difficult to administer is, Do those served grow as persons? Do they, while being served, become healthier, wiser, freer, more autonomous, more likely themselves to become servants? And, what is the effect on the least privileged in society; will they benefit, or, at least, not be further deprived.[12]

We may quibble over some of the words used, but his suggested outcomes are clearly in line with what we would hope to see as the outcomes of leadership in our churches and organisations.

A common response to the idea of servant-leadership is to ask, 'Where is the *leadership* in servant leadership?' To some people, it seems as if the task may be lost in taking care of relationships, and that such a style of leadership will be too laissez-faire, too indecisive and not directive enough. Servant-leadership is not a weak form of leadership. It is just as strong on vision; indeed, servant-leaders serve their congregations by taking time to discover what God wants them to do as a community. They will approach it differently, perhaps, with a greater emphasis on 'our vision' rather than 'my vision', and with discussion and input from all concerned as the vision is received and formulated. Furthermore, the implementation of the vision will not be top-down, with the leader as taskmaster, but more a collaborative effort in which each person has a part to play and the feeling is of a team at work.

Another fear is that servant leaders will be bullied by their congregations and, as one writer puts it, 'lose our individuality and become the football of others, kicked from one end of the church to the other'.[13] Certainly, servant-leaders will need to be assertive and to remember that they are serving God first, not people, or they may well be held to ransom by every awkward individual or tyrannised by every manipulator. To serve is not to be passive, and servant-leadership is not a convenient cover-up for cowardly behaviour. It takes courage to lead and wisdom to know when to hold our ground, and leaders must follow the example of Jesus in bravely confronting unacceptable behaviour. We serve our congregations best, sometimes, by standing firm and holding them to the noblest ways.

Power and service are to be held in creative tension. Servant leaders are not afraid of power but they exercise it cautiously and with restraint, and for the good of others. They are strong and confident in their leadership but unselfish at the same time. When someone uses power selfishly, they become a ruler or a tyrant. When someone is selfless but afraid of power, they become a doormat, a slave rather than a servant. Neither extreme is what we mean by servant leadership. Another writer, Dan Ebener, says:

The servant leader is powerful and unselfish. The servant leader uses power and service for the sake of the team or the organization. This contradicts two common notions about leadership in our culture: (a) that a person who serves others is not powerful and (b) that the person who uses power is self-serving.[14]

A third reservation about servant leadership is the danger that many people will ascribe to the idea but won't actually practise it. Placing the word 'servant' in front of 'leader' may sound very spiritual but may not mean much. Cross-cultural trainer Duane Elmer expresses his feelings clearly: 'Many who think of themselves as a servant-leader aren't—which amounts to self-deception. Many are tyrants, dictators, self-aggrandizers and benevolent oppressors. What passes for Christian leadership is rather shocking.'[15]

Elmer rightly says that the Bible speaks more about being a servant than it does about leadership, and that everyone is called to be a servant. He does agree, though, that every leader must show evidence of the essence of Jesus, which is humility, and that genuine servanthood is the basis for all leadership. 'If we servants emerge as leaders as well, let it be because people have seen the servant attitude and wish to affirm our giftedness. Then it won't be a role we have assigned ourselves but one honourably bestowed by others.'[16]

Reflection

- How would you define servant leadership? What has shaped your own approach to leadership, and how is it challenged by what Jesus says (and models) about leadership?
- What reservations do you have about servant leadership? How might it be misunderstood and misapplied?

9

Humility and the danger of pride

He will not shout or cry out, or raise his voice in the streets.
ISAIAH 42:2

Some time ago, I received a magazine from a national Christian organisation. The front cover was given over to the theme for that edition, the development of younger leaders. In bold capitals the heading proclaimed, 'Seven young leaders to watch out for', and beneath were pictures of each one, along with their names.

When I saw this I was incensed, thinking that this would expose them to the danger of pride. I felt it was wrong for a Christian magazine to be identifying up-and-coming 'stars' in this way, and I was already composing in my mind a letter to the editor to let him know what I thought. At the same time, I became aware that my reaction was a little over the top and a bit out of proportion. I have learned (slowly) over the years, when this happens, to stop and consider why I am annoyed. Thankfully I paused for thought and reflection.

As I pondered my reaction, I began to realise that the reason I was so annoyed was because I was not among the seven! Not that I could be described as an up-and-coming leader even then, but it had touched a nerve within me—the feeling that I had never been truly recognised within Christian circles. At the heart of the matter was my own pride and ambition, and it was not a pretty sight. The letter was never written.

Pride is the most deadly of sins because we are unaware of it ourselves, yet it lurks within every heart. It is the original sin in the sense that Lucifer, the brightest of all God's angels, was cast out of heaven for desiring the place of God (Isaiah 14:12–15). It is best described as 'selfish independence of God' but it has many manifestations, such as boasting and self-glorification, and is the root of many other sins as well.

The opposite of pride is humility, the quality that most characterises Jesus as the servant and that he most desires to see in his followers. Humility can be defined as 'dependence upon God' and also has many expressions, in particular the recognition that all we have is a gift from God and that we should give him the glory he deserves.

Jesus described himself as 'meek and lowly in heart' (Matthew 11:29, KJV). Meekness is humility expressed outwardly, in the way we relate to other people—with gentleness and forbearance, treating them with dignity and equality and recognising their intrinsic worth and value, while at the same time not feeling superior or insisting on our rights or trumpeting our accomplishments. It enables us to put the needs of others before our own and to fulfil Paul's injunction: 'Do nothing out of selfish ambition or vain conceit, but in humility consider others better than yourselves' (Philippians 2:3).

Lowliness is humility expressed inwardly, in the way we relate to God—an attitude of mind that is acutely aware of its dependency upon God. Jesus lived consciously from moment to moment in this disposition: 'The Son can do nothing by himself' (John 5:19; see also 7:16; 14:10). He lived only to bring glory to the Father and never for acclamation of his own: 'I am not seeking glory for myself' (8:50). From our perspective, we would add that lowliness includes a sense of our weakness, frailty and limitation.

Humility is the key characteristic of the servant portrayed by Isaiah and modelled by Jesus. It is a quality that Jesus longed to see formed within his disciples, because it is impossible to serve well without being humble. As we know, they struggled with their own pride and especially the desire for position. On three different occasions Jesus had to rebuke them for this (Mark 9:33–37; 10:35–45; Luke 22:24–30). The first time was at Capernaum, where they argued about who was the greatest. Jesus called them to him and said, 'If anyone wants to be first, he must be the very last, and the servant of all' (Mark 9:35). In other words, in the kingdom of God there is to be no emphasis on position or status, only on service. True greatness is defined not by how you rule but how you serve.

To make his point, Jesus invited a young child into their midst, welcoming the boy into his arms and saying, 'Whoever welcomes one of these little children in my name welcomes me; and whoever welcomes me does not welcome me but the one who sent me' (Mark 9:37). Those aiming to get to the top have no time for such trivialities. Those desperate to climb the ladder of success want to network with influential people of power, not babysit someone else's children! It is beneath their dignity, is messy and demanding, and will not benefit them in any way. Only a true servant would 'waste' their time on tiny tots, yet the way we treat the 'little people' reveals what is in our hearts and whether or not we are qualified for God's service.

This brings us to the words of Isaiah and his first statement concerning the character of the servant. Each of the three statements is expressed negatively, describing something that the servant will never do—in this case, 'shout or cry out, or raise his voice in the streets'. There are several ways to understand this, and, since each sheds a different light on the tension between pride and humility, we will consider them in turn.

The most obvious reading of these words is to understand them in terms of self-display and drawing attention to one's self, something uncharacteristic of the servant: 'He won't call attention to what he does with loud speeches and gaudy parades' (Isaiah 42:2, *THE MESSAGE*). This was something the Pharisees loved to do, however, standing on street corners and praying aloud so that they could be seen by passers-by, or even announcing their giving in the temple with loud trumpet blasts so that their generosity did not go unnoticed (Matthew 6:2–8). What should have been done in secret (and therefore in humility) was being done in public, out of pride. In similar vein, Jesus tells of the Pharisee who, praying in the temple, 'prayed about himself', reciting a long list of his good deeds. By contrast, a tax-collector, aware of his need, simply cried out, 'God, have mercy on me, a sinner.' He was the one who went home justified by God, 'for everyone who exalts himself will be humbled, and he who humbles himself will be exalted' (Luke 18:9–14).

The temptation to exalt one's self is very real. We all like to be noticed, to receive praise, to be recognised for our accomplishments. When that recognition is given to us unsolicited, we can receive it as an encouragement, as long as we don't allow it to swell our ego. More dangerous are the subtle (and not so subtle) ways in which we can promote ourselves and seek recognition without realising it—the Christmas newsletter, the 'testimony' at church, the posting on Facebook or Twitter, the story on our blog, the article in a magazine, the fishing for compliments, the little boastings in our conversations, and so on. What is important is to know our own heart, to be aware when something is causing us to feel proud, and to know how to keep ourselves humble.

True servants do not seek the praise of people and are content to allow God to determine their level of recognition. They are content to remain hidden and unknown, do not seek the limelight and feel no need to let others know of their importance or achievements. To be known and loved by God is sufficient, and to be recognised in heaven is reward enough. Like Jesus, they live for the Father's glory alone.

The second way of reading this verse is in terms of self-assertion, as defensive words of anger. This is how Matthew interprets it: 'He will not quarrel or cry out' (Matthew 12:19). Certainly the Hebrew words have a degree of violence about them. To shout is to shriek, to startle; to cry out suggests an attempt to dominate or shout others down; to raise the voice is to speak loudly enough to be heard some distance away. Commentator Samuel Carson says, 'As it is used here the expression carries the idea of people quarrelling in a house, and speaking so loudly, that what is said inside can be heard in the street outside.'[17]

We all know that pride manifests itself in a need to be right, a tendency to be argumentative and to have the last word. Religious people, in particular, find many things to fall out over and argue about, sometimes in unseemly and unloving ways. Paul tells Timothy clearly (and maybe with an echo of this verse in mind) that 'the Lord's servant must not quarrel; instead, he must be kind to everyone, able to teach, not resentful' (2 Timothy 2:24). He warns him several times about getting drawn into needless controversy (1 Timothy 6:3–5, 20; 2 Timothy 2:14, 23), which is always damaging.

One of the most destructive sins that I have encountered in church life is selfish ambition—that prideful desire to get to the top, to have power and influence over others. It is the kind of attitude that characterised Diotrephes, who, we are told, loved to be first, to have the place of pre-eminence (3 John 9). Selfish ambition always leads to quarrelling, since it creates competition and a jockeying for position (James 3:13–16). It can be disguised and rationalised but, sadly, within many church and mission leadership teams, strife is evident because selfish ambition is at work. Team members have never learned how to prefer one another in love (Romans 12:10), and the noise of their strife as they clamber for position can be heard down the street!

True servants, by contrast, feel no need to defend themselves. They can be assertive when necessary but seek to avoid being aggressive; they can stand for their beliefs without being argumentative or quarrelsome. They refuse to be drawn into power-plays or political manoeuvrings since they are not concerned with status or position. Like Jesus, they can remain silent even when misunderstood. Having been justified by God, they feel no need to justify themselves before people.

The third possible interpretation has to do with self-determination and the desire to go one's own way rather than God's.

In this case, the shouting is directed towards God and represents a rejection of his will and, in particular, of suffering. It is never easy to submit ourselves to God's will, especially when it seems that he is asking too much of us, and we may feel tempted to rail against him as the thief on the cross did (Luke 23:39). Human pride always finds it difficult to surrender control. It prefers that we demand our rights rather than meekly acquiesce.

For first-century slaves this was a pertinent issue, for they were often wrongly accused and suffered innocently. Peter called on them to live as servants of God, being respectful and submissive to all in authority, even unreasonable masters (1 Peter 2:13–17). Since they had very little right of appeal, his advice was to remain mindful of God's presence with them and God's pleasure in them as they suffered innocently. Indeed, they could see this as part of their calling: in suffering, they were following in Christ's footsteps, emulating his example, for he too suffered innocently (vv. 18–22). The suffering servant shows us how to respond in a godly way: 'When they hurled their insults at him, he did not retaliate; when he suffered, he made no threats. Instead, he entrusted himself to him who judges justly' (1 Peter 2:23).

Only a truly humble servant can walk such a path and can willingly submit to doing God's will, no matter what the cost. In these days of human rights and dislike of inconvenience, difficulty or hardship, this can be a hard message to communicate and to accept. Meekness is not weakness, however, and Jesus allowed himself to be led like a lamb to the slaughter not because he had no alternative but because he was consciously choosing, with great courage, to accept the assignment given to him (Isaiah 53:7).

The apostle Peter struggled with pride, being naturally out-spoken and self-confident, but, over the course of his lifetime, God dealt with him to make him a humble servant. At times he was humbled by God and at times he chose to humble himself. Speaking to a younger generation of leaders out of the wisdom of lived experience (see 1 Peter 5:1–7), he first reminds them that to be an overseer is to be a servant. This means that they should lead willingly because they are happy to serve, and should do so humbly, resisting the temptation to lord it over those they lead.

Next he encourages those who are younger (and therefore more prone to pride) to adopt a submissive attitude of the kind we have been describing, happily placing themselves under the authority of older leaders. He encourages the whole group to adopt a humble attitude to one another (some translations speak about 'wearing the apron of humility', an apt expression) because 'God opposes the proud but gives grace to the humble' (v. 5; Proverbs 3:34). I think this is a principle of God's activity that Peter knew from first-hand experience. When we allow pride to reign in our lives, we find that God gently resists us in order to humble us; when we walk humbly before him, we discover that his grace is flowing towards us and his blessing is on our lives. It is far better to be working with God than to have God working against us.

One of the most respected Christian leaders of recent times was the Anglican vicar and author, John Stott. Internationally known as a speaker and writer, Stott gave himself to developing other leaders and was known by countless people around the world whom he had mentored in some way, simply as 'Uncle John'. He epitomised the characteristics of the true servant in his humility and graciousness, and wrote this: 'At every stage of our Christian development and in every sphere of our Christian discipleship, pride is the great enemy and humility our greatest friend.'[18] This is a vital truth to remember as we seek to grow in our own servanthood.

Reflection

- How do you understand humility? Think about what it is and what it is not.
- Do you recognise any of these tendencies in yourself—self-display, self-assertion or self-determination? How can you make humility your friend?

10

Gentleness and the temptations of power

A bruised reed he will not break, and a smouldering wick he will not snuff out.

ISAIAH 42:3

The second characteristic of the servant concerns how he relates to others. The way we treat people—and especially the way we deal with weak and vulnerable people—reveals what is in our hearts. If we are operating out of a mindset of superiority and self-seeking, we may well respond with impatience and frustration; if we are motivated by love and compassion, our reaction will be one of care and concern. This characteristic is especially relevant to those who aspire to be servant-leaders.

The fact that Matthew brings the servant passage into the context of the healing ministry of Jesus (Matthew 12:15–21) shows how central the well-being of others is to the servant. Servant-leaders are not just concerned about their vision and the task before them. They do not see their followers simply as a means to achieving their goals or regard them as resources to be used, but are concerned to take care of them. In addition, while servant leaders must exercise power (we cannot lead without it), they exercise it wisely and for the benefit of those whom they serve. They lead with gentleness and are not heavy-handed.

This balance between power and compassion is brought out beautifully in an earlier section of Isaiah, which must surely inform our understanding of the servant's approach to leadership:

See, the Sovereign Lord comes with power, and his arm rules for him. See, his reward is with him, and his recompense accompanies him. He tends his flock like a shepherd: he gathers the lambs in his arms and carries them close to his heart; he gently leads those that have young. (Isaiah 40:10–11)

It is possible to be both powerful and tender, to lead clearly and decisively and yet care compassionately for those under our charge. Indeed, that is how God chooses to lead.

Some of the people we lead will be bruised, like a reed that has been trampled on. They will have been hurt by other people and wounded by the hard knocks of life. They will come to us from broken homes and failed marriages, and having been abused in any number of ways. They may feel disappointed with God and let down by the church, or be stressed by the demands of life and scarred by the spiritual battle. How we treat them is important. The servant leader will not take advantage of them or make their plight worse. With gentleness and understanding, the servant nurses them through to recovery.

Others will be exhausted, the flame of their zeal and enthusiasm having almost died out, like a candle about to be extinguished. They may have given themselves so fully to caring that they have nothing more to give. The demands upon them may have been so great that they feel they can carry no more. Their journey through life may have been so hard that they feel they cannot go a step further. Again, the servant-leader puts no additional pressure upon them and does not add to their burden. Instead, with loving understanding and wise counsel, she brings them back to restoration of health and vitality.

THE MESSAGE sums up the work of the servant like this: 'He won't brush aside the bruised and the hurt and he won't disregard the small and insignificant.' What a wonderful description of the ministry of Jesus! He was a 'powerful' man, teaching with authority, performing miraculous signs, followed by crowds of people, unafraid of challenging evil or hypocrisy wherever he saw it. Yet he dealt gently with people, welcoming the children, persevering with his disciples, elevating the place of women, welcoming tax collectors and sinners, reaching out his hand to disfigured lepers, healing the sick and feeding the poor.

Probably, no incident sums up this aspect of the character of Jesus more than his response to the woman caught in adultery (John 8:1–11). When other religious leaders would have had her stoned to death, he not only exposed their hypocrisy but showed compassion and understanding towards her, demonstrating her worth and value. 'Has no one condemned you?' he asked sensitively, and declared, 'Then neither do I condemn you.' Forgiven and accepted, she was free to live a new life—a bruised reed mended and a smouldering wick reignited. Here we see at work the healing power of grace, the hallmark of servant leadership—lifting burdens, not imposing them; helping people, not hurting them; developing others, not damaging them.

Many of us will know from personal experience that this is how Jesus treats his followers, and, as our great high priest, he continues to serve us in this way. The high priest of old was chosen simply because he could 'deal gently with those who are ignorant and are going astray, since he himself is subject to weakness' (Hebrews 5:2). As a sinner himself, he knew how to restore the fallen and encourage the defeated. Jesus has no such weakness (of sinfulness), but, having become a man and lived our life, he is well qualified to be a merciful and faithful priest for us: 'For we do not have a high priest who is unable to sympathise with our weaknesses, but we have one who has been tempted in every way, just as we are—yet was without sin' (Hebrews 4:15). What this means is that when we turn to him in our need, bruised and exhausted as we may be, we find a merciful response of welcome, acceptance and understanding; our cry is heard and we feel valued. Strengthening grace flows towards us yet again (v. 16).

What Jesus demonstrated by his example, he reinforced through his instruction of his disciples. He knew that power is an inevitable part of leadership but that it brings with it certain dangers, for power can always be misused, even innocently. We have already noted how the disciples struggled to come to terms with the new style of leadership that Jesus was introducing, which was so different from the style seen in the Pharisees or among the Gentile Romans. Their disputes about greatness continued right up to and during the last supper. Jesus was again firm with them: 'The kings of the Gentiles lord it over them; and those who exercise authority over them call themselves Benefactors. But you are not to be like that' (Luke 22:25–26).

Jesus was concerned not by the use of power but by its abuse. 'Lording it over' other people suggests a domineering attitude, in which the leader is seen as king and the followers are regarded as subjects to be told what to do. 'Exercising authority' in this context suggests a patronising attitude of superiority, where followers are looked down upon as being inadequate and inferior. It is not necessarily true that leaders deliberately act in this way; often they are unaware of how their actions are perceived and are perhaps unconscious of their own attitudes. Duane Elmer notes that while, among missionaries, the stated desire to serve is great, the oft-repeated conviction of nationals is that missionaries could serve better if they were not so superior. He confesses that he too has often unknowingly been guilty of a superior attitude, concluding, 'Superiority cloaked in a desire to serve is still superiority.'[19]

'I am among you as one who serves' (Luke 22:27) could have been taken as a motto by Jesus because it sums up his whole way of life. It is also the best protection against the misuse of any authority that we may have in leadership. Even at the last supper, Jesus served his disciples through breaking the bread and offering them the cup. The symbolism is almost as great as that of the washing of their feet, for the one who sits at table is usually the greater, but, once more, Jesus took the servant's role, demonstrating his alternative leadership style and declaring, 'The greatest among you should be like the youngest, and the one who rules like the one who serves' (v. 26).

This all seems straightforward enough but the reality is that, because of the insidious nature of power, it is not always handled well in churches, either by leaders or followers. A senior Baptist leader in England, Paul Beasley-Murray, was so concerned about the abuse of power that he undertook a research project into what was happening. He writes:

Sadly, time and again power has been misused and people have been abused in Christian churches and institutions. The travesty is that power has been exercised as if it were for God's sake... Many have been deeply wounded. The wounds have been so deep and the pain so intense that large numbers have let the church altogether... This experience of the abuse of power has been so devastating that many have given up on God altogether. [20]

I know from my own experience that this is true. During the early years of my Christian life, I was involved in an independent charismatic church that, looking back on it, was clearly abusive. I was in the leadership myself and, because I knew no better, was part of the abusive system of discipleship (sometimes described as 'heavy shepherding') that was in place. I have also had first-hand experience of the power that some large Christian organisations wield over their members, where the concerns of individuals are swamped by the closed nature of the system. Those in leadership positions are invariably supported by those above them, regardless of their behaviour, and there is no court of appeal for someone who feels mistreated. In my work as a retreat leader, I have met many who have been misused by mega-churches or mission agencies that seem to draw people in at one end and spew them out at the other, bruised and broken. This they do without any accountability or recognition of the problem. (For some thoughts on how to identify an abusive church or organisation, please see the Appendix.)

I am fully aware that leaders can be equally abused by congregations and that powerful individuals within churches can turn a minister's life into a living hell. My concern here, though, is with the responsibility of leaders to use power carefully, to handle it as servants. We must ask, therefore, why some leaders do become abusive. Assuming that their motives are not evil, why do they stray from the clear principles of servant-leadership?

In 2007, the World Evangelical Alliance Mission Commission published a report called *Worth Keeping*, which looked at missionary retention (how to keep missionaries effectively serving in their chosen countries). The report noted a clear connection between leadership issues and retention, with 'toxic' leadership cited as one of the main causes of unhappiness. It states:

Good, healthy leadership is quite distinct from poor, toxic leadership. The effect of the first frees people within the organisation to thrive, flourish, and give of their skills and resources effectively to the maximum benefit of the organisation. The effect of the second, the toxic leader, is to inhibit, hold back and severely limit the performance of their team. Long-term, a toxic leader will affect the individuals within the team, who themselves will experience inhibited growth and development.[21]

The report goes on to suggest that, while some toxic leaders are self-absorbed and egotistical, the majority are those who operate out of deep-seated inadequacy, causing them to behave selfishly and sometimes even deceitfully. They are not fully grounded in their identity in Christ and, in the terms of the Servant Song, do not know at the core of their being that they are 'chosen' and 'loved'. This insecurity means that they are easily threatened by others and become defensive; that they fear failure and overcompensate by becoming controlling; that they strive for success and are more concerned about how they themselves are doing than how others are developing.

I would certainly concur with that assessment but would add some other possible causes. Some leaders get carried away by their own success and think that the rules no longer apply to them. This is especially so with charismatic personalities who are outstandingly gifted and gather around themselves a large following of people who hang on to their every word. They are seldom challenged and begin to feel that every decision they make is right and every pronouncement is to be obeyed as if it were from God. Their success is the basis for their infallibility. Power is intoxicating and it is easy to become drunk on it or addicted to it, without even realising that this is what is happening. Followers can unwittingly become complicit in an abusive situation by placing leaders on pedestals and abdicating their own responsibility in decision-making and hearing the voice of God.

Other leaders are what we often call strong natural leaders, the 'field marshal' types. These people are strong on vision, high on commitment, bold in faith and unsympathetic to weakness. They forge ahead regardless in the name of God and often do not mind who gets hurt in the process. They confront disloyalty and are aggressive when challenged, so most people back off and a climate of fear prevails, in which the majority acquiesce for a quiet life. They achieve a great deal but the vision is considered more important than the people, so many are hurt in the process.

Some leaders are given a high power factor by the system in which they operate. They may have a senior position in an organisation that values loyalty and commitment, so their opinions are taken seriously and their decisions carry a great deal of weight. Sometimes scriptural passages about obeying leaders are cited (Hebrews 13:7, 17; 1 Thessalonians 5:12), but, while submission is a commendable quality, it is not to be given blindly or against one's conscience. Leaders who require unquestioning obedience or infer that to obey them is to obey God are on very dangerous ground. It takes a wise and humble person to exercise the degree of authority that is sometimes invested in leaders, and not all can handle it well.

Some abusive leaders behave in this way because they have been abused themselves, often in childhood. Having been treated harshly, they are determined to succeed in order to prove themselves—and often, through hard work and determination, they do so. Their weakness is that they do not know how to discipline appropriately and are often harsh in the way they treat people.

Because they drive themselves, they drive other people—but, while they themselves may thrive on a workaholic lifestyle, it is disastrous for the majority, and people around such leaders often experience burn out.

It should also be noted that demonic interference sometimes plays a part in abusive systems. Pride is a gateway for evil powers, and this is perhaps why God is so strongly opposed to pride when it comes to leadership. Those who allow themselves to think that they have created their own success, who feed on selfish ambition or feel that they need no outside help or accountability, are perhaps most vulnerable to this danger. Some Christians speak about a Jezebel spirit (1 Kings 18:4; 19:2; 21:7; especially 21:25; also Revelation 2:20), and, while we should be cautious about such identifications, even a sober thinker like Beasley-Murray recognises that spiritual 'powers' are sometimes at work.

What, then, are the marks of abusive systems? Generally speaking, there is a high degree of control and a low level of accountability or outside reference points. There may be a climate of fear and intimidation, together with a strong demand for conformity. Total commitment is required and, while much is asked in terms of time, money and energy, there is little sympathy for those who cannot keep up the pace. Often, a dominant personality will emerge to whom allegiance is given, almost in an idolatrous way.

How can we guard ourselves against such dangerous extremes? By modelling ourselves on Jesus, the servant-king. As long as our eyes are upon him and we are walking in his ways, we need not be afraid of being corrupted by power. If we make love our aim, maintain a humble disposition and take every opportunity to express our servanthood in practical ways, we will not go astray. When we treat people with respect, seek their best interests and minister grace to those around us, we will instead bring healing and restoration, proving ourselves to be true followers of Jesus.

Reflection

- 'I am among you as one who serves.' Meditate on these words of Jesus as you consider your own approach to leadership, to the exercise of power and authority, and to the way you treat those who bruised and broken.
- Is it possible to lead with gentleness? What would this mean in practice?

11

Faithfulness and the challenge of pain

In faithfulness he will bring forth justice; he will not
falter or be discouraged.

ISAIAH 42:3B–4

On 30 January 1887, the famous Baptist preacher C.H. Spurgeon
gave a sermon in London with the title 'Christ's work no failure'.
He based his thoughts on this part of the Servant Song, encouraging
his hearers with the thought that, since Christ's triumph was
assured, they would also know victory. He said:

*We are commended at all times to believe the Son of God. There is
never a season in which He is not a fit subject for contemplation and
expectation. But especially in cloudy and dark days ought we to behold
Him. Whatever He has undertaken, He will perform… I believe in the
final perseverance of the Lord Jesus Christ… We need not fail and be
discouraged, since He will not fail.*[22]

The third characteristic of the servant is stated more positively in
that it concerns his faithfulness to the task given to him. He will
indeed persevere despite difficulties and see it through to the end.
This task will not be without challenge, however, and suffering will
mark his pathway, as we have already seen. Yet he will not falter
(hesitate, draw back) or be discouraged (lose hope, want to give
up). He will not give way to self-pity.

The Hebrew text is interesting here, since verse 4 picks up the
words used in verse 3: 'falter' in the Hebrew connects with 'burn

low', and 'be discouraged' with 'bruise'. The implication seems to be that the servant finds himself under the same pressures as others, but without succumbing to them. He faces that which made others 'burn low' but he does not 'burn out'. He experiences that which 'bruised' others but he himself is not 'broken'. Alec Motyer comments, 'In context, the intention is not to say that the servant will be immune from suffering but only that the pressures and blows that immobilize others will not deter him. They will rather find him with adequate inner resources (*not falter*) and with a resilience against outward blows (*not... be discouraged*).'[23]

The challenge that comes to the servant in the course of his ministry is that of managing himself and coping with his own pain. He may be humble and self-effacing and may have a genuine love and concern for the people he serves, but can he handle his own emotions? He may be free of self-display and not given to heavy-handedness, but can he escape the grip of self-pity when things are not going well and he feels let down and disappointed? These are real questions for anyone, and especially for those in leadership. It is often said that the reason some people do not see success is that they give up too soon. They cannot deal with their pain and do not have the inner resources to make themselves resilient in the face of adversity. Put simply, they quit.

How does the servant manage to keep on keeping on? The first reason is that he is being divinely upheld (Isaiah 42:1). He is not left to his own resources but is receiving divine strength that is sufficient to carry him through every trial. He is dependent on God and knows how to draw on these resources when needed. He can be faithful because he has faith in God. This is spelled out in detail in verses 5–7, and we will be looking more deeply at the grounds of his confidence shortly. The second reason is that he has been given the Holy Spirit and allows the Spirit to minister to his inner needs. He is never alone or without help because the Comforter is with him (John 14:16–17), living within him and strengthening his inner being (Ephesians 3:16–17). He is fortified within against the storms that rage without. This is not to say that he does not struggle or feel low at times, only that he has the inner strength to keep on going.

When we apply all this to Jesus, we see again that it is a fitting description of him. According to the writer of Hebrews, he was 'faithful to the one who appointed him' and 'faithful as a son over God's house' (3:2, 6). His earthly life was full of challenges and, being fully human, he felt the pain of what he experienced, but he never gave up. He coped with his many years of obscurity in Galilee before his ministry began. He suffered the pain of family rejection (John 7:3–5) and of not being acknowledged in his home town (Mark 6:1–6). He managed to hold firm, despite tremendous hostility from the religious leaders of his day (John 5:16–18) and the disappointment of seeing his disciples struggling to grasp what he was teaching them (Matthew 15:16). He was the object of ferocious spiritual attack from the devil but stood his ground and resisted the most powerful temptations (Matthew 4:1–11). He must have been discouraged to see the rich young ruler walk away (Mark 10:21–22) and heartbroken at the news of his cousin John's beheading (Matthew 14:12–13) but he did not waver. Perhaps he struggled with the constant attention and lack of privacy (Mark 7:24; 9:30) but he doesn't appear to have become resentful or worn out by the intrusion.

Clearly Jesus knew how to resource himself. He was careful to withdraw to be with his Father and to be refreshed through communion with him (Mark 1:35). As a result, he lived with a sense of the divine presence (John 8:29). He nourished his soul through prayer, reading the scriptures and worship in the synagogue (Luke 4:16; 5:16). He maintained balance and perspective by reflecting on the joy that was set before him, allowing the future impact of his work to strengthen him in his present difficulty (Hebrews 12:2–3). He enjoyed the hospitality and friendship of Mary, Martha and Lazarus at Bethany (John 12:1–2) and benefited from the camaraderie of his disciples, despite their shortcomings (Luke 22:28). An occasional angelic visitor was appreciated, too! (Matthew 4:11).

This is not to say that everything was plain sailing, even for the Son of God. There were times when he might have faltered and given way to discouragement. John in particular helps us to see into the inner life of Jesus and to appreciate the intensity of his struggle:

- At the death of his dear friend Lazarus, he weeps and is affected deeply by Mary's pain: 'When Jesus saw her weeping, and the Jews who had come along with her also weeping, he was deeply moved in spirit and troubled' (John 11:33).
- When he begins to realise that it is time to go towards Jerusalem for the final time, he has to steel himself for what lies ahead: 'Now my heart is troubled, and what shall I say? "Father, save me from this hour"? No, it was for this very reason I came to this hour. Father, glorify your name!' (12:27–28)
- When he becomes aware that Judas, one of the Twelve, will betray him, he is deeply hurt: 'After he had said this, Jesus was troubled in spirit and testified, "I tell you the truth, one of you is going to betray me"' (13:21).

What we see recorded here is no surface emotion. This is deep pain, revealing major disturbances within him that might easily have thrown him off track—but they didn't. His resolve to do the Father's will remained intact.

It is in the garden of Gethsemane that Jesus faces his ultimate struggle, and he is not afraid to reveal his anguish to the disciples: 'Then he said to them, "My soul is overwhelmed with sorrow to the point of death"' (Matthew 26:38). He likens the suffering that awaits him to the drinking of a cup, and he is not sure if he can go through with it. Using the most intimate of terms to address God, he prays, 'Abba, Father, everything is possible for you. Take this cup from me.' Finally comes the moment of absolute surrender: 'Yet not what I will, but what you will' (Mark 14:36). This is the moment when the battle for faithfulness is won, but the victory is hard fought.

A most beautiful commentary on this holy moment is given by Henri Nouwen:

Why then could he still say yes? I can't fully answer that question, except to say that beyond all the abandonment experienced in body and mind Jesus still had a spiritual bond with the one he called Abba. He possessed a trust beyond betrayal, a surrender beyond despair, a love beyond all fears. This intimacy beyond all human intimacies made it possible for Jesus to allow the request to let the cup pass him by become a prayer directed to the one who had called him 'My Beloved'. Notwithstanding his anguish, that bond of love had not been broken. It couldn't be felt in the body, nor thought through in the mind. But it was there, beyond all feelings and thoughts, and it maintained the spiritual communion underneath all disruptions. It was that spiritual sinew, that intimate communion with his Father, that made him hold on to the cup and pray: 'My Father, let it be as you, not I, would have it' (Matthew 26:39).[24]

What about ourselves as we seek to follow in his steps and serve the Lord? Jesus never hid the cost of following from his disciples: with him there was no small print. 'Remember the words I spoke to you,' he said: '"No servant is greater than his master." If they persecuted me, they will persecute you also' (John 15:20; 13:16). He expressed the cost of discipleship in terms of denying ourselves and taking up our cross to follow him. In other words, the path of obedience will require that we put God first in our lives and are willing to make sacrifices in order to fulfil his purpose for us.

This radical obedience to the Father's will took Jesus to Calvary, and it may involve a kind of death for us as well. It may be that, in fulfilling the call of God upon their lives, a few will be called to martyrdom. Some will give their lives by serving in remote and hostile places, succumbing to disease or sickness, traffic accident or violent attack. These will be the minority. For most of us, it will be the kind of death we experience as we give up our own ambitions and comfortable lifestyles and choose to serve God wherever he calls us, doing whatever task he assigns to us.

This kind of dying involves a spiritual principle that must be understood by any who want to serve the Lord. Jesus expressed it like this: 'I tell you the truth, unless a grain of wheat falls to the ground and dies, it remains only a single seed. But if it dies, it produces many seeds. The man who loves his life will lose it, while the man who hates his life in this world will keep it for eternal life' (John 12:24–25). His point is that there can be no spiritual fruitfulness or effectiveness in service without a willingness to suffer. Only when seeds enter the ground and 'die' can the life within them be released and multiplied fruitfulness occur. It is a law of nature and of spiritual life. There are no short cuts to this, and no easier ways. Each of us will have our own cup to drink, if we are willing, for this is the way of the servant: 'Whoever serves me must also follow me; and where I am, my servant also will be. My Father will honour the one who serves me' (v. 26). It is when we feel the pain of obedience that we may ourselves be tempted to quit.

I have not always found it easy to follow Jesus, and there have been times in my own life when I have shed tears and wanted to give up. I have faltered and been discouraged and felt that I could not carry on. I have been both a bruised reed and a smouldering wick. Yet something held me when I had no strength of my own; a 'spiritual sinew' (to use Nouwen's phrase) bound me to Jesus when I might easily have quit. He remained faithful when I might have proved faithless, and the grip of grace kept me from falling. He healed my wounds and fanned into flame the gift of God within me.

We can never tell when a day of testing will come to us, but we can send our roots deep into Christ so that, when the wind of adversity blows our way, we are not blown over. We cannot control the storms of life but we can build our lives on the solid rock of intimacy with Christ so that, when we are shaken, we do not collapse. Just as Jesus lived his life in God, so we can develop inner strength and resilience through abiding in Christ. Like him, we can find strength through spiritual friendships and times of corporate worship.

Spurgeon concluded his sermon with an exhortation to his hearers: 'I want you to eject at the back door every suggestion that enters your house as to the defeat of Christ and the future of the gospel; it is not possible, it cannot be.'[25] It is a timely reminder for those of us who seek to serve God in a very different world from his: God is still on the throne and his purposes will come to pass, no matter what the outlook. It reminds us of an earlier, apostolic injunction of equal relevance to every servant of God: 'Therefore, my dear brothers, stand firm. Let nothing move you. Always give yourself fully to the work of the Lord, because you know that your labour in the Lord is not in vain' (1 Corinthians 15:58). What is required of servants, above all, is that they be found faithful.

Reflection

- What pain are you experiencing in your own life right now? How are you dealing with it?
- How does the example of Jesus encourage you? How can you strengthen yourself so that you remain faithful?

The
Servant's
Confidence

12

The God who speaks

This is what God the Lord says—the Creator of the
heavens, who stretches them out, who spreads out the
earth with all that springs from it, who gives breath to
its people, and life to those who walk on it.

ISAIAH 42:5

Confidence is a vital ingredient in any kind of performance. It is
well known in sport, for example, that if a player's confidence is
high, they will do considerably better than if their confidence is
low. In soccer, if a striker is having a good run and scoring regularly,
more of his shots will be on target than if he is on a poor run
and hasn't scored for several games. It is the same in life, and with
ministry. If we have confidence, we will live with greater joy and
freedom and will serve with greater vitality and effectiveness. If we
are lacking in confidence, life will be a struggle and ministry will be
hard work.

As we move into the second part of the Servant Song, we notice
a significant difference. In the first part, the Father was speaking
about the servant; in the second part he is speaking to the servant.
Description has become address, and we are now able to listen
in on the words spoken directly to the servant as he begins his
work. It seems clear that the Lord is speaking in order to encourage
his servant, for he has promised to uphold him. Confidence in
ministry is not self-confidence; it is confidence in our relationship
with God and in his ability to sustain us.

As I prepared to write this chapter, I did some background
research on why people drop out of ministry. I came across some

statistics from America that really saddened me.[26] They are from a survey of more than 1000 ministers, carried out in 2005–2006, and reflect a general pattern reported in other surveys in different parts of the world. Here's what I discovered:

- 90 per cent said they were frequently fatigued.
- 89 per cent had considered leaving the ministry.
- 57 per cent would leave if they could find a better job.
- 77 per cent didn't have a good marriage.
- 75 per cent felt inadequately trained.
- 71 per cent battled depression.
- 38 per cent were divorced or in the process of divorcing.

As I read and pondered this article and thought back to my own experience of church leadership, I felt a huge compassion welling up within me for these unknown people. Behind these figures are real lives full of pain and hurt. These are people who have felt God's call to ministry, who are walking the path of servanthood and are themselves best described as bruised reeds and smouldering wicks. As I reflected further, I felt I began to understand why God speaks in this way at this point in the song: he too feels compassion for such dear people, and in a much greater way than I could ever do, for he is their God. He longs to uphold them.

What is true of people in church ministry is true of people in cross-cultural ministry and of people serving God in secular occupations: we all find it tough and need encouragement. God is aware of us, though, and knows our situations, and he wants to speak words to reassure and strengthen us.

We will examine shortly the three confidence-building promises that God makes to his servant in this passage, but first we need to remind ourselves of who exactly is speaking: it is God the Lord. This is important because many of us will have experienced empty promises from people who either had no intention of keeping their word or did not have the resources or ability to carry them out. God the Lord, however, can be trusted because of his character (faithful and true) and because of who he is (the Lord, Creator of heaven and earth). He is 'not a man, that he should lie' (Numbers 23:19). As the psalmist said, 'The word of the Lord is right and true; he is faithful in all he does' (Psalm 33:4).

Notice how the Lord introduces himself. He is the Creator God, the one who brought everything that exists into being by his word of power (Hebrews 11:3). He created the heavens above, stretching them out like a canopy or a blanket, putting the stars in place and giving them their names, causing the sun to rule the day and the moon the night (Psalm 136:7–9; 147:4; Isaiah 40:22). When we stand before the sky at night, we are humbled by its vastness, awed by its beauty, and amazed at its order and structure. It is the God who designed and made all this who speaks to us.

He is the one who created the earth and everything that springs from it. In his wisdom he laid the earth's foundation and made the sea, the dry land and every living thing, whether plants or animals (Psalm 104). When we look around us and see the evidence of his handiwork, and when we meditate on his powerful deeds in creation, we can be sustained by the knowledge that the Lord is 'faithful to all his promises and loving toward all he has made' (Psalm 145:13).

What is more, he is the one who made each one of us, giving us the very breath we breathe and sustaining us every day of our lives. When we consider our own createdness, we realise that we are 'fearfully and wonderfully made', made for his purpose and known through and through (Psalm 139:13–16). As our Maker, he understands what makes us tick and is aware of our limitations (Psalm 103:14). So the Servant can say, 'Before I was born he called me; from my birth he has made mention of my name' (Isaiah 49:1). When he speaks to us, it is going to be with complete accuracy, knowing who we are and being aware of our circumstances.

We must notice here two things about the word that this Creator God speaks. First, it has creative power. It brings things into being and accomplishes the purpose for which he speaks it forth. The psalmist says, 'For he spoke, and it came to be; he commanded, and it stood firm' (Psalm 33:9). Isaiah agrees:

As the rain and the snow come down from heaven, and do not return to it without watering the earth and making it bud and flourish, so that it yields seed for the sower and bread for the eater, so is my word that goes out from my mouth: it will not return to me empty, but will accomplish what I desire and achieve the purpose for which I sent it. (Isaiah 55:10–11)

Paul often thought of the work of salvation as a second creative act of God: 'For God, who said, "Let light shine out of darkness," made his light shine in our hearts to give us the light of the knowledge of the glory of God in the face of Jesus Christ' (2 Corinthians 4:6). Thus, when God speaks to us personally, we can be sure that his word will be effective. It will be creative in our lives and circumstances and make a difference.

Second, it has sustaining power. It releases the breath (or life) of God into us, building us up in our inner being and strengthening our faith. When we receive it by faith, it does something to us. It acts upon us in a way that gives life to us. Daniel experienced this invigorating effect of God's word: 'When he spoke to me, I was strengthened' (Daniel 10:19). So did Ezekiel at the start of his ministry: 'As he spoke, the Spirit came into me and raised me to my feet, and I heard him speaking to me' (Ezekiel 2:2). It was the testimony of some unknown Old Testament saints that when they were sick and cried out to God for help, 'he sent forth his word and healed them' (Psalm 107:20). When God speaks to us, therefore, we will be fortified for the task he has given us. His life will come into us and we will be made to stand up again.

When we look at the earthly life of Jesus, the true servant, we see that the Father also spoke to him in this way. Jesus was aware of the truth that 'man does not live on bread alone, but on every word that comes from the mouth of God' (Matthew 4:4; Deuteronomy 8:3). What sustained him in his ministry was the word that came from the Father. We have already noted how the Father spoke words of affirmation and reassurance to him at his baptism and during the transfiguration (Matthew 3:17; 17:5), but there was a third occasion when the heavenly voice was heard.

It came shortly after Jesus' triumphal entry into Jerusalem, when the realisation that the hour had come for him to die was pressing in upon him. He was deeply disturbed but offered himself afresh to God: 'Now my heart is troubled, and what shall I say? "Father, save me from this hour"? No, it was for this very reason I came to this hour. Father, glorify your name!' (John 12:27–28). Immediately there was a response from heaven: 'Then a voice came from heaven, "I have glorified it, and will glorify it again." The crowd that was there and heard it said it had thundered; others said an angel had spoken to him' (John 12:28–29). Even though this voice was primarily for the benefit of the onlookers, it would certainly have strengthened Jesus and he would have welcomed its reassurance. It is encouraging for us to know that he too needed to draw strength from God, and that the Father spoke to him when it was necessary.

When God speaks to us, we do not normally hear an audible voice. The most common way that God speaks to us is through scripture, when the Holy Spirit takes something written in the Bible and applies it to us personally. It may be in the course of our regular reading through the Bible, as we are listening to scripture being expounded or even as we are reading a book like this. It is as if a specific sentence leaps off the page, speaking directly to our circumstances and being made alive to us in a deeply personal way. Jesus said that his sheep know (recognise) his voice (John 10:27), and it is one of the marks of all believers that they can hear God speaking to them, in particular through scripture.

A second way in which God may speak to us is through the gift of prophecy. This is when God uses the words of another person to address us directly. This gift is explained for us in 1 Corinthians 14 and can be exercised in a number of different ways. Sometimes, in preaching, the speaker will say something that exactly fits the circumstances of one of the listeners, but without any prior knowledge. It could be that a person is given something in the context of a meeting that they feel is from God but meant for a particular person. Alternatively they may be led by the Spirit to share something directly with an individual—a verse of scripture, a specific thought or a mental picture of some kind.

All prophecy like this has to be carefully considered to see if it is from God and should never be accepted blindly, however persuasive the person may be. A good test is to see if it is line with what God has already been saying to us and if it brings peace to our hearts as we listen to it. What it should always do is to accomplish God's purpose: 'those who prophesy speak to people for their strengthening, encouragement and comfort' (1 Corinthians 14:3, TNIV). God uses prophecy to build us up, not to tear us down.

The third way in which God commonly speaks to us is through what is often called 'the witness of the Spirit'. Once we have come to know God personally, he is able to speak to us directly—heart to heart, as it were. The human spirit has the ability to recognise the voice of God and, with time, we begin to discern when God is speaking to us. It begins with the assurance of our salvation: 'The Spirit himself testifies with our spirit that we are God's children' (Romans 8:16). We know intuitively, within ourselves, that we belong to him and he is our Father. As we grow in our relationship with God, this ability to recognise when he is speaking to us becomes stronger, although we may sometimes still be uncertain and occasionally get it wrong.

The writer to the Hebrews reminds us that God speaks 'at many times and in various ways' (Hebrews 1:1). This widens considerably the number of different ways in which God may speak to us. If we are alert to him, his voice is everywhere. We hear it in creation, of course, both in the big picture of its splendid grandeur and in parables of nature—insights into God's mind that we recognise in the things we see and notice, as did Jeremiah with the almond tree (Jeremiah 1:11–15) or Moses with the burning bush (Exodus 3:1–6). Equally, God can speak to us through a piece of music, a film we are watching, an article we are reading, an interview we hear, the words of another person and so on.

What we are seeing here, then, is both the willingness of God to speak to us in our need and our ability to hear his voice when he does speak. When God speaks, he does so in power and to good effect, and when we receive his word, we are strengthened in our faith and further equipped for our task. This inner dialogue is one of the main ways in which God upholds his servants, and it is important that we develop our ability to listen to God and receive his word. God is aware that ministry is not easy and knows we may feel discouraged and downhearted. In the midst of our struggles he wants to reassure and strengthen us.

I can look back to a time in my own ministry when I was deeply discouraged and about to give up. I was in pastoral work at the time and, like some of those mentioned in the survey, already mulling over in my mind what I would do next. I had an outside speaking engagement one Sunday evening that I attended with little enthusiasm, wondering if it would be my last such engagement. I delivered my message as best I could, and then somewhat reluctantly went to shake hands with people as they left the meeting. It was there that, to my surprise, God spoke to me.

A gentleman whom I didn't know shared with me some words of encouragement. I cannot remember now exactly what he said and he will never know what his words meant to me, but, as he spoke, there came into my soul a glimmer of hope. His words were not dressed up as prophecy and he didn't share a verse of scripture with me; he simply passed on his appreciation for what I had shared that night, but through his words God spoke to me. It was a turning point, and I found strength and grace to carry on. I had been upheld.

We will be turning our attention now in some detail to the three promises given to the servant in these verses:

- 'I will take hold of your hand.'
- 'I will keep you.'
- 'I will make you to be.'

Each promise deals with a specific area of challenge that we face as we seek to serve God. It may be that, if you are discouraged, God will speak a word of life to you as you read through these chapters. I pray so. It may be that you are in a period of stability and things are going well; if so, store away these promises for future reference, for the day will inevitably come when you will need them.

Reflection

- Recall any ways in which God has spoken to you in the past. How did he speak to you? What did he say, and how did it help you?
- Become conscious that God has not forgotten you in your struggles. He is aware of you and knows your need for reassurance. You are his servant; he has chosen you and delights in you, and will uphold you. Allow him to speak to you and do not be afraid to receive his word when it comes.

13

God's presence to reassure

'I, the Lord, have called you in righteousness; I will
take hold of your hand.'
ISAIAH 42:6

Just before my wife and I went out to Borneo as young missionaries
in 1975, one of her elderly aunts presented me with a beautiful
leather Bible. She had written in the front a greeting, along with the
words of 1 Thessalonians 5:24: 'The one who calls you is faithful
and he will do it.' At the time, I thought it was no more than a 'nice'
verse, appropriate enough but nothing too significant. However,
as the years have passed by and my experience in ministry has
deepened, I now realise how foundational these words are.

We have seen already that the servant is one who is called. He
is not a volunteer enthusiastically offering himself to do God's
work, but someone whom God has chosen: 'I have called you
in righteousness.' This awareness of having been 'called' by God
should undergird our service for God. He calls people 'in righteousness', which I take to mean in the integrity of who he is—a
good and just, kind and gracious Master. What this means is that
if he gives someone a particular calling, he will provide all that
they need and will sustain them so that they can accomplish the
purpose for which he has called them.

It is of utmost importance, therefore, that we know we have
been called by God. All believers have been called in terms of
salvation (see, for example, Romans 1:6–7), and all are called to
follow him in discipleship (for example, 1 Peter 2:9), but God calls
some people to particular tasks and responsibilities. This may or

may not require us to leave ordinary employment behind and be 'full-time'. What matters is that we realise that the work we do has been given us by God. Two things follow from this conviction:

- The recognition that it is God's work, and that 'he will do it'. This sounds straightforward enough but, in practice, it is not so easy. The work quickly becomes 'my' work and we take on the responsibility for it, often trying too hard and ending up burnt out through our own efforts to do what only God can do. One of the major lessons of Christian ministry comes as we realise that it is God's work and learn to allow him to work through us.[27]
- The belief that because it is God's work, God will be faithful to us in providing all the resources we need to accomplish the task. We can confidently look to him for provision and the supply of all our needs.

It is in the context of this calling that God makes to his servants three 'very great and precious' promises, to quote 2 Peter 1:4. The first of these—'I will take hold of your hand'—is a promise of divine presence in the midst of our fears and anxieties. This is something in which God takes the initiative, reaching out to us and, metaphorically speaking, taking us by the hand. We are held in the grip of grace. This promise is repeated throughout the scriptures in various ways.

King David, on the run in the desert from his enemies, found comfort in the midst of a sleepless night: 'On my bed I remember you; I think of you through the watches of the night… My soul clings to you; your right hand upholds me' (Psalm 63:6, 8). This was in accordance with the promise given to him by God: 'I have found David my servant; with sacred oil I have anointed him. My hand will sustain him; surely my arm will strengthen him' (89:20–21). Asaph records the experience of someone going through a time of doubt and questioning and yet knowing the nearness of God: 'Yet I am always with you; you hold me by my right hand' (73:23).

Most of us will remember, as children, the reassurance we received from being able to hold the hand of our mother or father—for instance, on the first day at school or on a visit to the dentist. That is one of the main reasons for holding hands. It communicates warmth and presence, and offers us comfort and reassurance. It reminds us that we are not alone. Of course, we quickly grow out of the need to hold a parent's hand. All too quickly, children grow up to become independent and, by the time they are teenagers, they often do not even want to be seen with their parents, let alone be holding their hand. As adults, especially if we are men, we come to the place where we say defiantly, 'I don't need anyone to hold my hand!'

This proud, self-sufficient display of independence may last for a time, but most of us realise as we go through life that we do need outside help, even divine assistance. Life has a way of throwing up challenges we didn't expect, making us realise that we are not as self-sufficient as we thought. Ministry life is the same. Often we feel out of our depth, inadequate and unable to cope, even overwhelmed by fears and anxiety. There is nothing unusual in this. Indeed, as the psychologist Paul Tournier wrote, 'All men, in fact, are weak. All are weak because all are afraid.'[28]

It was Tournier's contention that, among human beings, there are only two reactions to this inner distress: strong reactions and weak reactions. Those who are 'strong' conceal their fear with bravado and a mask of self-assurance, inspiring fear in others while cleverly hiding their true feelings from them. Those who are 'weak' cannot conceal their anxiety. They become flustered and nervous, almost paralysed by their fear and easily dominated by the strong. According to Tournier, however, it is the weak who are the most honest. It does take a certain degree of courage to admit vulnerability and that we need a helping hand, even when the hand is the hand of God. When we are no longer afraid to admit our weakness, though, we have arrived at a healthy place spiritually.

As well as being a sign of reassurance, taking someone's hand can be a measure of friendship and even intimacy. I am often involved in cross-cultural training for those going to work in Africa, and we always emphasise the importance of greeting people and of holding hands while doing so. This is something very new for most Western men, so we make them practise holding the hand of another man while sharing a conversation—something that is a real mark of friendship and acceptance in the places where they will be working. It seems strange at first, but they get used to it eventually. Similarly, holding the hand of someone of the opposite sex is often the first sign of love and communicates a degree of attraction and intimacy. Westerners are more familiar with the significance of such a gesture and appreciate the power of loving touch.

We have seen consistently that Jesus is the pattern for our own servanthood and, as we read the Gospels, we see again and again how he allowed the Father to strengthen him. He lived in a close and intimate relationship with him, finding companionship and comfort with the Father at times when he could have been extremely lonely or afraid. 'The one who sent me is with me,' he said; 'he has not left me alone, for I always do what pleases him' (John 8:29). The Father's presence was real to him; he felt the reassuring touch of his hand upon his shoulder.

Isolation is one of the great challenges of Christian ministry. Some people are called to serve God in places that are physically isolated: they are far removed from the comforts of their own language and culture and have few friends with whom they can share deeply. Those in leadership positions know how lonely it can be when you carry the burden of responsibility for others, have to make difficult decisions and often have to hold confidential information that is hard to bear alone. It is important that, like Jesus, we develop an intimate relationship with the Father and allow him to minister to us in our need.

I often think of Paul as a rugged individual, self-contained and highly resilient in the face of much adversity. This is partly true but, in the closing section of what may have been his last letter (2 Timothy 4:9–18), he shows a deep vulnerability and need for companionship. Imprisoned for his faith, he is clearly feeling iso-lated, lonely and fragile. He has been badly let down by Demas and has seen his good friends Crescens, Titus and Tychicus move on to other places. Luke is still with him but he longs to see Timothy and Mark again, urging them to come quickly. He feels under-resourced, too, needing some good books to read, something to write on and a cloak to keep him warm. He is still stinging from his conflict with Alexander, hurting on the inside. Most worryingly, he wonders what the outcome of his trial will be, and it seems that everyone has deserted him. Generally speaking, he is feeling pretty miserable and let down.

But Paul is not alone, and into his misery and loneliness steps the friend who sticks closer than any human being could ever do (Proverbs 18:24). He states what happened simply, yet powerfully: 'But the Lord stood at my side and gave me strength, so that through me the message might be fully proclaimed and all the Gentiles might hear it' (2 Timothy 4:17). We are not told how this happened. It might have been through a vision, a dream in the night or an angelic appearance; it could have been simply a strong assurance welling up within his spirit. What we do know, though, is that the Lord who had called him did not abandon his servant but stood by him in his moment of greatest need.

What does it mean, then, when scripture says that the Lord will take hold of our hand? It is best understood as a metaphor for the empowering presence of God that comes to us, lifting us out of fear and anxiety, loneliness and despair. Sometimes it will come to us in a spiritual way, as it did to Paul. Most often, though, it seems to me, God comes to us in a human way, through other people whom he uses to bring us comfort, reassurance and the strength to carry on. This was the way in which Jesus came to the two friends on the Emmaus road. They were deeply downhearted and disillusioned, almost ready to give up, when 'Jesus himself came up and walked along with them' (Luke 24:15). He knew they were in pain and came to find them in their need. He offered them his divine friendship, and, once they had invited him into their home, their eyes were opened and their hearts uplifted.

Tan Soo-Inn is the director of a ministry in Singapore committed to promoting spiritual friendship, the kind of relationship in which we experience both the human and divine aspects of friendship. He says that 'the best human friendships should mediate the friendship of God',[29] and encourages each of us to develop relationship with one or two others who can fulfil that role in our lives. His appreciation of the role of spiritual friendship comes out of his own painful experience.

Having been a successful church leader, Soo-Inn found himself in a spiritual wilderness that began with the death of his wife from cancer in 1993. One tragedy led to another, and a second marriage ended in divorce. He lost most of his public ministry and went into clinical depression. He was no longer able to carry out his ministry but had to continue to function as a single parent, trying his best to raise his two boys. He says candidly:

Looking back on that period of my life, I often wonder how I survived. In truth, I know the answer—I survived because of the grace of God and the encouragement of my friends. It is in your darkest moments that you discover who your true friends really are, and that God's friendship is faithful and sure.[30]

In my own work I do a lot of international travelling and the schedule is often very demanding. Sometimes, when one trip seems to merge into another (and I have not followed my own advice in leaving enough recovery time between trips), I can feel overwhelmed and drained of energy, wondering how I can possibly fulfil my next assignment. On one such occasion, I happened to share how I was feeling with a friend, and she sent me a beautifully crafted prayer (she is great with words). I was so moved by this little prayer that I made it into a bookmark and took it with me. The words sustained me then and have done so since. I now keep it in the front of my Bible. This was the prayer:

Father as I go, please go with me.
My weariness and heavy heart I leave with Thee.
And pour your mighty Spirit, Lord, to overflow my being—
And flood with light my tired mind, and fill my soul with singing!

Underneath it I added a verse from Isaiah that seemed appropriate: 'I am he, I am he who will sustain you. I have made you and I will carry you; I will sustain you and I will rescue you' (Isaiah 46:4).

When God has called us to a task, he has called us in righteousness, in the integrity of who he is. He will not fail us or forsake us. We can lean hard upon him and expect him to provide for us and sustain us. We can listen carefully for his voice, knowing that he will speak to reassure and calm us, and we can allow him to take us by the hand and lead us on.

Reflection

- 'The one who calls you is faithful, and he will do it.' Meditate on this verse and apply it to your life right now—especially in the light of any fears or anxieties, doubts or insecurities.
- Think about how God often meets our need for reassurance through other people. Who might be a help to you? Who might you be able to help?

14
God's protection to guard

'I will keep you.'
ISAIAH 42:6

An experienced Christian leader in Australia, who regularly mentors
other leaders throughout the country, has an interesting question
that he sometimes asks his mentees: 'If Satan was going to take you
out of ministry, from your experience, how would he be likely to
do it?'[31]

That kind of question really puts us on the spot, doesn't it? It
awakens us to the reality that Satan wants to render us ineffective
in the work that God has given us to do, and it asks us to be on
our guard against his schemes. It requires us to know ourselves
well enough to be aware of our own weakness and vulnerability,
as well as to recognise Satan's most likely strategy against us. The
devil is aware that if you strike the shepherd, the sheep will be
scattered (Matthew 26:31), and that is why leaders come under
particular scrutiny from the enemy of our souls. One fallen leader
will produce many disillusioned and dispirited followers.

The second promise given to the servant is the simplest, being
only four short words, but perhaps it is the most important. It
reminds us that God is able to keep us through temptation and
trial so that we can complete our task and accomplish our purpose.
He is the Lord, our keeper (Psalm 121:5, KJV), or, as THE MESSAGE
has it, our Guardian God, attentively watching over us to protect us
and deliver us. Our confidence is not in ourselves but in him. Like
Paul, we can expect to finish well because he is with us (2 Timothy
4:7).

The ability of God to keep his people was enshrined in Israel's consciousness through the Aaronic blessing, which the high priest was to pray over the people. It begins with the words, 'The Lord bless you and keep you' (Numbers 6:24). It became a central thought in the spiritual perspective of godly individuals, expressed beautifully in the heartfelt prayer, 'Keep me safe, O God, for in you I take refuge' (Psalm 16:1). Even King David, warrior that he was, reminded himself that it was God's protection that mattered: 'For in the day of trouble he will keep me safe in his dwelling; he will hide me in the shelter of his tabernacle and set me high upon a rock' (27:5). Isaiah, speaking prophetically on God's behalf, says,

When you pass through the waters, I will be with you; and when you pass through the rivers, they will not sweep over you. When you walk through the fire, you will not be burned; the flames will not set you ablaze. For I am the Lord, your God, the Holy One of Israel, your Saviour. (Isaiah 43:2–3)

When we consider the challenges that come to us as servants of God, that threaten the successful accomplishment of our calling, we think of two key issues—temptations and trials—both of which can render us ineffective or shipwreck our faith altogether. You will know from personal experience (just as I do) how difficult it can be to navigate a way through the choppy waters that these two storm centres create in our lives. You will also know friends and colleagues who, to your surprise and sadness, did not come through their time of testing. None of us, however experienced or mature, can afford to be complacent, for we know that Satan is always looking for an opportunity to trip us up (1 Peter 5:8).

We will consider the issue of temptation first. Scripture is clear that we are bound to face temptation (Matthew 18:7). It is not that God tempts us but that sinful desires are still resident within us, and, given the right circumstances, a chain reaction of desire can be triggered within us, leading us to sin (James 1:13–15). Further, Satan is described as the tempter and he knows exactly how to exploit any weakness that he finds in us (Matthew 4:3; 1 Thessalonians 3:5). Even though we have the Holy Spirit to help us and we know the word of God intimately, if we find ourselves tired and lonely, angry or depressed, and not on our guard, we are all vulnerable to temptation.

Some years ago, Richard Foster wrote about what I regard as Satan's three main avenues of attack, in his book *Money, Sex and Power*. None of these is wrong in themselves but, historically, they have formed the battleground of personal holiness. 'The crying need today,' he wrote, 'is for people of faith to live faithfully. This is true in all spheres of human existence, but it is particularly true with reference to money, sex and power.'[32] Speaking metaphorically, Foster describes the 'demon' that lurks beside each one of these powerful forces: the demon in money is greed, the demon in sex is lust, and the demon in power is pride.

The Bible (and Jesus in particular) has a lot to say about money, most notably that we cannot serve God and Mammon (the spiritual power behind materialism) and that the love of money is the root of all evil (Matthew 6:24; 1 Timothy 6:9–10). Greed seems to be at the heart of so much of the world's economic woes, while serious gambling has become a leisure activity encouraged by many governments. Assuming we have avoided the obvious traps of stealing and dealing dishonestly, it is always helpful to consider the place that money has in our lives, how we use it and how it influences our behaviour and decision-making. We may discover that we are more materialistic than we thought, less generous than we would like to be, and gaining far too much of our security from our own accumulation of wealth. Even the lack of money can bring a snare, leading us away from contentment and into an unhelpful anxiety or resentful griping.

Scripture is very positive in its approach to sex, seeing it as one of God's good gifts to us, to be exercised responsibly and joyfully within the context of marriage. Nowadays, in the West, almost all the accepted standards of Christian morality have been overturned and many Christians are in a dilemma about how they should express their sexuality. The temptation to immorality is stronger than ever because ungodly behaviour seems so normal. It is the virgin who is abnormal, the faithful spouse who is naive. Experimentation is recommended and freedom of expression encouraged. In such a context, Christians must establish clear boundaries in all their relationships, know when they are most vulnerable and, like Joseph, know how to 'flee' when temptation beckons (1 Corinthians 6:18). A moment's pleasure can cost a hard-won reputation; a foolish choice can destroy a lifetime's work.

The danger is not only in what is done. These days, because of internet access, the potential impact on our thought-lives is greater than ever. The rise of the pornographic industry is staggering and the easy availability of hard-core porn is alarming. Those who feel lonely or have unmet intimacy needs are particularly vulnerable to this secret and hidden danger. Because it doesn't appear to affect other people directly, it can be justified as harmless fun, but of course it is degrading both to those who take part and those who watch.

The dangers of power, we have already discussed, but, because it is such a destructive force and so contrary to true servanthood, it is worth another brief mention. What is so dangerous about power is that it can masquerade as 'real' leadership—that which is forthright and clear, bold and visionary. Our models of leadership may be based so closely on the models we see in society that we do not recognise the danger of using Christian leadership as a vehicle for our own drive for success and need to make a mark. The potential for pride that lurks within the exercise of all power and authority can make us blind to the way we treat others and deal with them. It takes a humble person to handle power well.

Power is at the heart of leadership and we must be aware of its corrupting effect. Whatever power or authority we have over those we lead must be handled carefully and must have a strong ethical basis to it—for example, the conviction that the best use of power is to empower others, and that power should never be used to belittle others, bully them or take advantage of them in any way. It requires us constantly to remind ourselves that we have been entrusted with the influence that power brings, and that we are answerable to God for the way we use it.

The temptations behind money, sex and power are interrelated and affect us all, young and old, male and female. They are found in churches and Christian organisations, among ministers and missionaries, in monasteries and suburban homes. Times of stress seem to make us especially vulnerable. From his work in talking with and listening to church leaders, Keith Farmer notes a pattern:

In general, the process is as follows: the stresses of leadership—such as criticism, people leaving the church, and lack of effective boundaries—lead to very negative self-talk. For example, the leader may say to themselves, 'I am a failure as a leader.' This in turn leads to compensatory behaviour of a self-indulgent and/or addictive nature. Examples are pornography, gluttony, and overconsumption of alcohol.[33]

How does God keep us when we are facing temptation? Paul supplies part of the answer:

So, if you think you are standing firm, be careful that you don't fall! No temptation has seized you except what is common to man. And God is faithful; he will not let you be tempted beyond what you can bear. But when you are tempted, he will also provide a way out so that you can stand up under it.' (1 Corinthians 10:12–13)

We can see here five steps to overcoming temptation:

- Stay humble and remember that without God's help you are vulnerable.
- Don't blame yourself for feeling the pull of temptation: it is part of our common humanity and God is aware of your weakness.
- Believe that God will be faithful to you: he knows the limit you can bear, and will not allow you to be tempted beyond it. You are able to resist and you do have the strength to do so, however weak you may feel or however strong the temptation.

- Look for the way of escape that is always there—saying 'No', avoiding a compromising situation, being accountable to a close friend, not exposing yourself to danger and so on.
- Expect to be victorious and, when you have come through, give the glory to God.

This is not to say that it will be easy. Many of us will fight a real battle with temptation and it will take every fibre of our spiritual muscle to overcome, but it can be done.

The second threat to the successful fulfilment of our calling comes in the form of trials, the challenging events that life throws at us, with the potential to destabilise our faith and make us want to give up. Again, we should not be surprised that we are exposed to the hardships of life in a fallen world in the same way that others are. Paul warned his new converts, 'We must go through many hardships to enter the kingdom of God' (Acts 14:22). He himself experienced a painful 'thorn in the flesh' and suffered a whole catalogue of painful events, including beatings, imprisonment, shipwreck, hunger and thirst, sleepless nights and homelessness, risks to his life and the stress of looking after the churches in his care (2 Corinthians 11:23–29; 12: 7–10).

The clearest understanding of the nature and purpose of trials is given to us by James, the brother of Jesus. He writes, 'Consider it pure joy, my brothers, whenever you face trials of many kinds, because you know that the testing of your faith develops perseverance. Perseverance must finish its work so that you may be mature and complete, not lacking anything' (James 1:2–4). Trials come in many shapes and sizes and take many different forms. For example, they might be practical (things breaking down, shortages of funds, lack of premises, inadequate infrastructure), physical (health issues, tiredness, accidents, opposition), emotional (relationship difficulties, dealing with conflict, worries about family, feelings of inadequacy, stress, living in another culture), spiritual (oppression from the enemy, difficulties in prayer, feeling far from God, lack of visible results) or mental (the constant burden of responsibility, decision-making, developing strategy and making plans).

All these complications challenge our faith, forcing us to ask searching questions: 'Is God really with me? Am I doing the right thing? Can I cope with this?' What is happening, though, is that God is using the difficulties to stretch our faith and thereby to strengthen it. Faith must be exercised, and trials provide the opportunity for us to show that we will trust in God even when things are not going well. In this way we learn to persevere—that is, to keep going for a sustained period. The more we persevere, the more we grow in our faith, and this helps us to become mature—the kind of people who are steadfast and immovable, always giving themselves to God's work (1 Corinthians 15:58). These are the kind of people that God can use most effectively.

Perseverance is not a joyless, dull, dutiful characteristic. It is actually joyful because, through it, we see beyond the present pain and comfort to the bigger picture, appreciating what God is working in us. Bible commentator Derek Tidball notes:

We respond with joy because we know some of the deeper issues involved, which helps us to interpret suffering not as the miserably negative force which others perceive it to be, but as an instrument in the hands of a sovereign, wise and gracious God using it for our good. It is a call to put God into the whole picture of life; the bad times as well as the good.[34]

Peter adds to our understanding by recognising the purifying effect that trials have on our faith. Trials deliver us from a shallow, self-centred reliance on ourselves, in which we are tempted to use God for our own ends, into a faith that allows us truly to depend on him and seek his glory above all. They present us with a kind of test that gives us the opportunity to prove the reality of our faith. Peter says:

In this you greatly rejoice, though now for a little while you may have had to suffer grief in all kinds of trials. These have come so that your faith—of greater worth than gold, which perishes even though refined by fire—may be proved genuine and may result in praise, glory and honour when Jesus Christ is revealed. (1 Peter 1:6–7)

How, then, does God mediate his help to us? Firstly, through the ministry of Jesus, our merciful and faithful high priest. Jesus himself was tempted by the devil in the wilderness (Matthew 4:1–11). His temptations were real and powerful, yet he resisted the devil and did not sin. Having been tempted as a human being and having overcome, he is now able to communicate to us the grace and strength that we need to have victory in the midst of our own temptations and trials:

For we do not have a high priest who is unable to sympathise with our weaknesses, but we have one who has been tempted in every way, just as we are—yet was without sin. Let us then approach the throne of grace with confidence, so that we may receive mercy and find grace to help us in our time of need. (Hebrews 4:15–16)

Seated now at the right hand of the Father, the risen Jesus is praying for his church, and his intercession is powerful in its effect (Hebrews 7:23–25). Just as he was aware of Peter's trial and prayed for him, so he is aware of our need and prays for us (Luke 22:31–32). What is more, as we cry out to him for help, he hears our prayers and pours his grace into our lives, releasing his strength into our weakness (2 Corinthians 12:9).

The help of God is mediated to us, secondly, through the people around us—those who care for our well-being and are wise enough to know when we need a little support. We saw in the previous chapter how valuable it is to have soul friends, people who come alongside to help and encourage us. Many people find it helpful also to have a mentor, an individual who knows them well and walks with them through the challenging periods of life, to whom they hold themselves accountable. Such a person offers a non-threatening and accepting presence, a prayerful friendship, a listening ear and some wise counsel. They provide a context for honesty and openness, help us to establish good boundaries and ask the kind of questions that keep us on track.

Well-known American pastor Mark Driscoll has testified to the help he received from such a person, a man called Dave Kraft. He writes:

A few years back I was basically burned out in every way. The combination of the fast growth of the church, my lack of experience, and the immaturity of our organisational structures left me completely over-extended. I was working out of my area of gifting, and it was literally breaking me, though I was only in my mid-thirties. My adrenal glands were fatigued. I could not sleep. I was seriously discouraged, exhausted, and frustrated.

Kraft was one of several older leaders who helped Driscoll to get his life and ministry in better order. He took him through a formal mentoring process and gave him permission to make some tough decisions for the well-being of his family and the church he led. 'A few years later,' says Driscoll, 'I can easily say I am in the best season of my life.' [35]

It is not God's will that we fail to complete the assignment he has given us. He wants us to succeed and has promised us his help. He is able to keep us from the power of temptation and in the pressure of trial. We can be kept by the power of God (1 Peter 1:5).

Reflection

- Consider the question with which this chapter began: 'If Satan was going to take you out of ministry, from your experience, how would he be likely to do it?' How would you answer that question honestly?
- Think about ways in which you can strengthen yourself against temptation and in times of trial. In particular, be aware of ways in which you can reinforce yourself in areas where you are vulnerable. If you need help, don't be afraid to ask for it.

15

God's purpose to guide

'I will keep you and will make you to be a covenant for the people and a light for the Gentiles, to open eyes that are blind, to free captives from prison and to release from the dungeon those who sit in darkness.'

ISAIAH 42:6–7

The third promise given to the servant is the largest promise in that its scope has an impact not only on the servant but also on those who will benefit from his ministry. It is a promise about inner change and transformation that leads to outer effectiveness, and speaks about the kind of difference that only a Creator God can make. The one who made us in the past is the one who continues to make us in the present, shaping us with the future in mind.

This ongoing creative work of God is also recognised in the second Servant Song. There we read, 'He made my mouth like a sharpened sword, in the shadow of his hand he hid me; he made me into a polished arrow and concealed me in his quiver' (Isaiah 49:2). This suggests a process of preparation and equipping for the task ahead, being made fit for purpose over the course of a lifetime. There is a natural development and growth taking place within the servant by which he is made ready for his work. This activity of God has a private side to it (hidden and concealed) but a public outcome (sharpened sword and polished arrow).

When we look at the life of Jesus, we see a similar pattern at work. The first 30 years were the hidden years when he stayed in the obscurity of Nazareth, employed as an ordinary carpenter. We know that during his childhood he was subjected to the normal stages of growth and development: 'And the child grew and became strong; he was filled with wisdom, and the grace of God was upon him' (Luke 2:40). Here we see development in three areas—physical, intellectual and spiritual. Jesus had to grow like everyone else: his mind had to develop and his spirit had to mature. These years of concealment provided the preparation for ministry that really only began when he was about 30. Even then, I would suggest, he continued to learn how to work in harmony with the Father and with the Spirit, and to continue to walk the path of obedience as the Father's will became clearer.

The Gospels reveal a similar process taking place in the lives of the disciples. Jesus called them with this in mind: '"Come, follow me," Jesus said, "and I will make you fishers of men"' (Mark 1:17). Right from the start, he made it clear that this would be an apprenticeship where they would learn by being with him, watching him in action and listening to his teaching. It would be a transforming friendship, and his purpose was to prepare them to continue his work when he had returned to the Father.

I can look back now over 40 years of ministry and see this same developmental process at work in my own life. I have grown and developed as a person, and I trust I have grown and developed in ministry. I am certainly conscious of how God has shaped and formed me during my past, preparing me for what I am doing now. I am also conscious that he is still at work in me, getting me ready for whatever lies ahead, and that I am far from being a finished article. This is the way God works, and I am sure that you are conscious of it as well.

The work of transformation that God is doing in each of his children has two outcomes in view: character and competency. His first aim is to make us like Jesus, so that we display a Christ-like character. The second is to equip us for ministry, to enable us to serve him effectively. The two are linked together, of course. We will be more effective in Christian ministry when we show a Christ-likeness in the way we behave, and our involvement in the challenges of ministry will help in the formation of our character.

We will look first at the development of character, something to which we have already given considerable attention. God's priority is to make us like his Son, and this is the purpose for which he called us in the first place (Romans 8:28–29). It is something that he does but with which we cooperate, not just passively but actively—welcoming the changes he wants to bring to our lives and intentionally seeking transformation. The life of Christ is best understood in terms of the fruit of the Spirit: love, joy, peace, patience, kindness, goodness, faithfulness, gentleness and self-control (Galatians 5:22–23). When these qualities are seen in us on a consistent basis, then we are becoming like Christ. But how does it happen?

I believe there are six aspects to this inner transformation, like the six points of the Star of David. Think of this star as one triangle inverted and placed on top of another. The first triangle represents what God does as he works in us, and the second triangle is what we do as we cooperate with the process of transformation.

What does God do?

- He works in us by the Holy Spirit, who is the agent of change. The Spirit shows us where we are not like Christ but also imparts the life of Christ to us so that we can change. He gives us the desire to be like Jesus and the power to break free from unhelpful patterns of behaviour.
- He speaks to us through the scriptures, which provide the pattern for change, showing us a new way of living and giving us an understanding of his will for our lives. Through the Gospels we can see what Jesus was like, and through the epistles we learn that he lives within us.
- He orchestrates the circumstances of our lives so that our pride is humbled and we learn to depend on him. Through trials and difficulty, he shapes our character and bends our will. This is the context of change.

What do we do?

- We practise the spiritual disciplines, by which we place ourselves in the way of grace. We study the Bible, spend time in prayer, take part in Christian community, worship, practise giving, serve other people and so on, all as a way of drawing closer to God and expressing our faith. These disciplines provide the means of change.
- We spend time alone in personal reflection, examining our lives before God, listening to his voice and receiving his love into our hearts. We seek to know ourselves as people and to understand who we are in Christ. This is the method of change.
- We meet with others who are passionate for God, soul friends with whom we share our faith journey and, perhaps, a mentor or spiritual director to advise us. We are open and vulnerable, allowing these trusted friends to give us feedback and help us become more self-aware. Their example inspires us to be the best that we can be. Here we find the motivation for change.

This is a lifelong process, of course, and most of us have days when we feel we are doing well and other days when we despair of ourselves. On the whole, though, if we give ourselves to the process, change will be taking place. We may not always be aware of what is happening because true goodness is always unselfconscious, but others will be able to see the difference that God is making in our lives. It is the people closest to us who will be best placed to assess our progress in Christ-likeness.

Next we will look at competency, the ability to do the job that God has given us to do. Most of us will feel very inadequate and under-skilled and will empathise with Paul in his cry, 'Who is equal to such a task?' (2 Corinthians 2:16). We will often feel out of our depth and out of our comfort zone, but the good news is that the Creator God has promised to make us able for whatever he asks us to do.

When we look at what is spoken to the servant in Isaiah, we see that the promise is expanded to say that he will be made to be a covenant for the people. This could be said only of Jesus, the true servant, and in fact it highlights a significant part of his ministry. God had promised through the prophet Jeremiah that he would bring into being a new covenant (Jeremiah 31:31–34), and this happened through the death of Jesus on the cross.

We saw earlier that one aspect of the cross was that it fulfilled the demands of the law and made it possible for us to be justified. A second outcome is that a new covenant was inaugurated, providing us with a better way of drawing near to God. His sacrificial death was far more effective than the animal sacrifices of the old order. Hebrews puts it like this: 'For this reason Christ is the mediator of a new covenant, that those who are called may receive the promised eternal inheritance—now that he has died as a ransom to set them free from the sins committed under the first covenant' (Hebrews 9:15). Christian ministry is based upon this new covenant. Jesus is the guarantee of it (7:22) and he is the reason why it is much superior to the old way (8:6). He is also the mediator of it—the one who brings it into being and applies the benefits of it to people, and on a worldwide basis. The servant becomes a light to the Gentiles. The result is that blind eyes are opened and captives set free. The new covenant is powerful and effective.

Whether our calling is to proclaim the gospel of justification from sin or to demonstrate the compassionate justice of the kingdom, or a mixture of both, what we do must flow from the dynamics of the new covenant. Our confidence stems from the fact that we have confidence in this new way of relating to God. We know that it works and can be trusted. Paul summarised his ministry in these terms:

Such confidence as this is ours through Christ before God. Not that we are competent in ourselves to claim anything for ourselves, but our competence comes from God. He has made us competent as ministers of a new covenant—not of the letter but of the Spirit; for the letter kills, but the Spirit gives life. (2 Corinthiams 3:4–6)

Here we have the basis for all effective ministry. The word translated 'ministers' is the Greek word *diakonos*, 'meaning servant'. We serve people, whether through proclamation or demonstration, by offering them the opportunity of relationship with God on the basis of what Christ has done on the cross. This is not about rules and regulations ('the letter') but about the life of Christ within us ('the Spirit'). As we share this wonderful invitation, the Spirit empowers us, anointing our words and actions and making them powerful channels of God's life to others. Those who receive the message of our words and our deeds receive the gift of salvation. It is the gospel itself that has power. As Paul says elsewhere, 'I am not ashamed of the gospel, because it is the power of God for the salvation of everyone who believes: first for the Jew, then for the Gentile' (Romans 1:16).

God is in the process of making us increasingly confident in the gospel and in our understanding of how to work in collaboration with him. He is shaping us and moulding us so that we become better channels of his grace. It is not that we feel more powerful in ourselves. Probably the opposite is true. The more God uses us, the more inadequate we feel, but he is at work 'making us to be' more spiritually competent. For this to happen, he may need to work deeply within us. This is where character and competency overlap and the inner and outer journeys intersect.

I like the illustration that Alan Jamieson uses in his book about becoming 'an instrument shaped to the contours of the hand of God'. This, he suggests, is the ultimate purpose of the transforming work in our lives, bringing us to the place where we become willing and useful instruments in the purposes of God. 'We become,' he says, 'instruments that God has fashioned and prepared for his personal use.'[36] When we think of a butcher's knife, a writer's pen or a carpenter's chisel, we realise that these chosen tools are not necessarily the newest or the most expensive but the ones that, through constant wear and usage, become a perfect fit for the hand of the user. Likewise, God is constantly shaping our lives so that we can be an instrument of choice in his hand.

As with the development of Christ-likeness, so with the growth of spiritual competency there is something that God does and something we do in response. He is acting upon us by his Spirit but we are required to make room for his working in our lives. Paul expressed it in terms of a household:

In a large house there are articles not only of gold and silver, but also of wood and clay; some are for special purposes and some for common use. Those who cleanse themselves from the latter will be instruments for special purposes, made holy, useful to the Master and prepared to do any good work. (2 Timothy 2:20–21)

Here we see that our part is not only to make ourselves available for God to use but also to separate ourselves from anything that would prevent him from using us. We have to choose to keep our lives free from anything that would restrict our usefulness to God, and have the godly ambition to be the best that we can be for him. There is a price to be paid in terms of personal sacrifice.

Whatever the nature of the ministry that God gives us, if it is based on the new covenant and inspired by the Spirit it will have the effects described here by Isaiah:

- It will bring light instead of darkness—the knowledge of God replacing the ignorance of unbelief, fear and superstition.
- It will give freedom instead of bondage—liberating those who live under the rule of sin, in the grip of powerful addictions or in subjection to demonic powers.
- It will offer hope instead of despair—releasing people from the gloom of depression, the futility of life without God and the emptiness of having no purpose or meaning in life.

To be involved in such a ministry is a great blessing, and to be used by God to bring the benefits of the cross into people's lives is an enormous privilege. Any sacrifice we make or suffering we endure seems worthwhile when we consider the outcome.

As I write this, I cannot help but think of a couple supported by our church for work in Africa. They went into cross-cultural ministry later in life but have done an amazing job in one of the poorest parts of the country where they work. They have managed to combine clear gospel proclamation with several projects that demonstrate God's love. Along with their African co-workers, they have established churches in a number of villages in an area dominated by witchcraft. They have regularly provided food distribution and established foster care for orphans and are now in the process of developing a farm to grow food, teach good practice and provide a training facility for church leaders. None of this has been without great struggle.

They have coped with riots, economic meltdown, constant fuel shortages, lack of regular power supply, travel on treacherous roads and the general challenges of life in Africa. They have been encouraged by some of the new believers and deeply disappointed with others. They have been separated from their children and isolated from their friends. They have been sick and exhausted and, at times, close to giving up, and yet they have persevered and are doing a remarkable work. They are typical of so many unsung heroes of the gospel, quietly getting on with kingdom business in hidden parts of the world: no fuss, no fanfare, just humble service for Jesus.

What keeps this couple, and many like them, going? What will keep you and me going? The promises of God. His presence in our moments of fear and despair; his power in our moments of temptation and testing; and his purpose being worked out in our lives, deepening our characters and making us competent. There is no other explanation for such bravery and resilience. It has to be God.

Reflection

- As you think about your life, how has God been at work in you to develop your character? How is he shaping and forming you? Are you cooperating with him or resisting his work in you?

- Think about this scripture: 'Our competence comes from God.' How does this speak to you and how does it point you to the true source of power and effectiveness in ministry?

The Servant's Attentiveness

16
Listening and responding

'I am the Lord; that is my name! I will not yield my
glory to another or my praise to idols. See, the former
things have taken place, and new things I declare;
before they spring into being I announce them to you.'

ISAIAH 42:8–9

Perhaps the most important quality of a servant is attentiveness.
A servant learns how to anticipate the master's will by watching,
listening and anticipating his desires and then responding discreetly
and with the minimum of fuss. It is as the psalmist describes it: 'As
the eyes of slaves look to the hand of their master, as the eyes of a
maid look to the hand of her mistress, so our eyes look to the Lord
our God till he shows us his mercy' (Psalm 123:2).

As we near the end of our journey through the first Servant Song,
we come to the point where we begin to ask ourselves the question,
'How shall I apply this to my life?' For some, this will be the first
time of taking seriously the implications of the call to servanthood.
For most, for whom servanthood is already established as the basis
of their lives, it will provide the opportunity to stop and pause and
ask this pertinent question again. All of us will want to consider if
God want us to continue doing what we are already doing or if he
has something new for us to do. The answer will be found as we
learn to listen attentively to what he is saying and as we keep our
eyes on him so that we can respond to any direction he may give
us.

The God who has spoken to reassure the servant now speaks
to guide him. Part of our confidence in God is the knowledge that

when we need guidance he will speak to us: 'Whether you turn to the right or to the left, your ears will hear a voice behind you, saying, "This is the way; walk in it"' (Isaiah 30:21). It is God's responsibility to make his will clear to us, and we can relax as we seek to discern what he is saying. Like the boy Samuel, who was told to go and lie down as he waited for God to speak, we too can rest in the assurance that God is well able to make his purpose known to us. Our responsibility is to maintain the attitude of heart that says, 'Speak, Lord, for your servant is listening' (see 1 Samuel 3:1–10).

This section begins with a very strong declaration: 'I am the Lord; that is my name.' The servant is left in no doubt as to who is in charge here—it is the Creator God, whose purposes are being worked out in the earth and whom the servant is called to obey. Everything starts with God. He is the source of everything, and the servant does well to remember that. Our lives are meant to revolve around God, not vice versa. As created beings, we are made to live for his glory and to do his will. This is how we find our own true happiness and sense of purpose. Rick Warren, author of the famous *Purpose-Driven Life*, emphasised this at the start of his book. 'It's not about you,' he began. 'If you want to know why you were placed on this planet, you must begin with God. You were born *by* his purpose and *for* his purpose... It is only in God that we discover our origin, our identity, our meaning, our purpose, our significance, and our destiny.'[37]

According to the Westminster Shorter Confession (1647), the 'chief end of man' is to glorify God and enjoy him for ever. We glorify God by worshipping him. This is what we were made for, and the worship of heaven reflects this great truth: 'You are worthy, our Lord and God, to receive glory and honour and power, for you created all things, and by your will they were created and have their being' (Revelation 4:11). We glorify God by doing his will. According to Paul, this is why God has saved us: 'It's in Christ that we find out who we are and what we are living for. Long before we first heard of Christ and got our hopes up, he had his eye on us, had designs on us for glorious living, part of the overall purpose he is working out in everything and everyone' (Ephesians 1:11, THE MESSAGE).

The giving of glory to God is fiercely contested, however, and in two ways. Firstly, sinful men and women do not always want to give glory to God, preferring to seek their own glory and live for their own ends. This is why Paul says that to sin is to fall short of the glory of God (Romans 3:23), since its essence is a prideful self-centredness. Secondly, Satan seeks to rob God of his glory and become the object of worship himself (Matthew 4:8–9). He seeks to lead men and women away from devotion to God by offering them counterfeit religion. These two strands (human rebellion and Satan's ambition) come together in an elaborately constructed alternative to the worship of God—idolatry. Here is the heart of the spiritual battle and the reason for the determined stance of God, who says, 'I will not give my glory to another or my praise to idols' (Isaiah 42:8).

Throughout the Old Testament, idolatry was the downfall of the people of Israel. Time and again, despite all the demonstrations of God's love and power, they became ensnared by the fertility gods of Canaanite worship. All the prophets spoke out against the futility of idolatry, but Isaiah is perhaps the most scathing in his denunciations. Idols cannot be compared to the true and living God. They are man-made objects crafted from perishable material, who cannot see or talk or understand. They have to be carried around because they cannot walk, and nailed down lest they topple over. How can they save anybody? (See Isaiah 40:18–20; 41:7; 44:9–20; 46:5–7.)

There is one way in particular by which the falsity of idols is demonstrated and the superiority of God confirmed: they cannot speak and they certainly cannot predict the future. Through his prophets, God had announced beforehand that the nation would be defeated and the people taken into exile. Now, In Isaiah's day, he is speaking again to say that they will be restored to their own land, and the temple and city of Jerusalem will be rebuilt: 'Who foretold this long ago, who declared it from the distant past?' asks the Lord mockingly of the useless idols. ''Was it not I, the Lord? And there is no God apart from me, a righteous God and a Saviour; there is none but me' (Isaiah 45:21).

The servant, by contrast, is one who lives for the glory of God, and through his witness many others will turn from idolatry to worship God alone. Although technically it is outside of the Servant Song as defined by Bernard Duhm, Isaiah goes on to record a psalm of praise that arises as God defeats his enemies (42:10–13). Once again, God is to be worshipped as he deserves: 'Let the people... sing for joy; let them shout from the mountaintops. Let them give glory to the Lord and proclaim his praise in the islands' (vv. 11–12).

Any review of our service for God must bring us back to the foundational truth that our lives are to be lived for the glory of God. We do not live for ourselves—our own ambition, success, advantage—but for God. If we lose sight of this, it may be hard to discern God's will for the future. We need to come back to the place where we are ready and willing to do whatever he asks of us. 'Living the rest of your life for the glory of God,' says Warren, 'will require a change in your priorities, your schedule, your relationships, and everything else.'[38] No matter how long we have been on the road of discipleship, this needs to be our ongoing disposition. Jesus could say, 'I have brought you glory on earth by completing the work you gave me to do' (John 17:4). Paul summarised it like this: 'So whether you eat or drink or whatever you do, do it all for the glory of God' (1 Corinthians 10:31).

As we open up ourselves for God to speak to us, we can take confidence from our own history with God. Just as the people of Israel could look back to times when God had spoken and his word had come true, so we can take note of our own story with God. 'See, the former things have taken place' is what God says to us as well. Several passages of scripture recall the faithfulness of God to Israel, usually despite their failures (Nehemiah 9:5–37; Psalm 105—107; Acts 7:1–53), and it is worth looking back over our own past to see how God has been at work in our imperfect lives. Such reminders of God's goodness serve as springboards for future steps of faith and obedience. Remembering how God led us, provided for us and enabled us in days gone by is not simply spiritual nostalgia. It is a way of giving glory to God, stimulating faith for the present and providing a context in which we can hear his voice for today.

Salvation history is not just a personal thing. It is just as important to be aware of how God has led us as communities of faith or as Christian organisations. Quite recently, the church to which I belong celebrated its 20th anniversary. A small group of us who have been involved since it began got together to plan a weekend of celebration. As we reminisced about the early days, we became really thankful for all that God has done through us. We are still only a small church and it has been tough going at times, but to stop and consider the number of people who have been helped by the church, the impact we have had in the community and the many answers to prayer we have seen gave us fresh impetus to carry on with the work God has given us to do.

For several years, Evelyn and I were members of the Overseas Missionary Fellowship (OMF). This is an organisation with long spiritual roots, going back to its founder Hudson Taylor and the work in China in the late 19th century. One of the reasons we joined the mission was because of the impact upon us of his life story, especially his faith and commitment to God. It was a constant source of encouragement to us, as we served in South-East Asia, to be aware of the many examples of God's faithfulness and miraculous provision in the history of OMF and to experience it for ourselves. Those early years of being grounded in the faithfulness of God have continued to inspire us and give us confidence for other steps of faith. As you consider the history of your church, mission or organisation, allow its story to speak to you today.

If God can speak to us through our past, he can certainly speak to us about our future, revealing to us what lies ahead. God is a dynamic God and is always at work in the world. This means that the purpose he has for us is an unfolding one, and we must be open to change and ready for any new assignment. Just as one phase of the life of service comes to an end, a new phase opens up before us, and God is always preparing us for the next step.

It is a characteristic of the work of God that it is organic, by which I mean that it operates in a similar way to nature. Things tend to happen gradually, and things come to pass slowly. God is seldom in a hurry. The things that God is doing 'spring into being', which suggests that they burst out from their hiddenness like bulbs do in springtime. There is an appointed time; we have to wait for that time to come, and we cannot make it happen any faster. There is a great need for patience, as every farmer knows. The germination of seeds cannot be hurried. Timing is everything in God's work.

All the same, God does not leave us completely in the dark. He often announces things beforehand. Occasionally he does this with a fanfare and it is clearly stated and obvious to all. It may be through a prophetic word that is given to us or prayed over us, as was the case with Timothy at the start of his ministry (1 Timothy 1:18) or Paul as he went up to Jerusalem (Acts 21:10–11). Sometimes it will be through a combination of the natural and supernatural—as when Paul and his companions were prevented from going into Asia and Bithynia by the Spirit but were moved to enter Macedonia by a vision, concluding together that this was God's leading (16:6–10). Often it will come through reasoned discussion and sensitive listening to God, as at the Jerusalem Council, where they could say, 'It seemed good to the Holy Spirit and to us…' (15:28).

At other times we will be guided more by what we might call inklings, little impressions in our spirit of what could be the way ahead, tentative notions of what may be about to happen. Often this gentle guidance cannot be explained easily to others; it is just something we know intuitively and we have to wait for the assurance to grow within us and further confirmation to be given. This is like what happened with Nehemiah as he prayed for several days over the plight of Jerusalem. Gradually he became convinced that he himself had to do something about the situation. God had planted a seed in his heart. Later on, his tentative guidance was confirmed when the king granted him permission to go to Jerusalem and also provided the materials he needed (see Nehemiah 1:4—2:9).

Sometimes, in the process of review, we come to the conclusion that we should continue doing what we are already doing, perhaps with slight changes but also with a renewed enthusiasm and vision. Irish bishop Ken Clarke tells how, on a trip to Uganda, he was invited by his host bishop to spend some time on their Prayer Mountain, a retreat centre belonging to the Anglican diocese of Nebbi in the north-west of the country. Arriving near the summit, he was surprised when his host disappeared to pray alone, leaving Ken to his own devices. Initially he was somewhat nervous, his imagination running wild with thoughts of armed rebels, wild animals and poisonous snakes, but after a while he settled into a time of seeking God.

In the busyness of his church responsibilities at home, it had been a while since he had spent time like this, and it proved to be invaluable. He returned from the remote location with a renewed sense of God's call upon his life. 'Through praying, praising, interceding, and reading the Bible (which was all I had with me), I knew God had spoken something into my life,' he writes.[39] He had been reminded of the words of Isaiah 50:4, part of the third Servant Song: 'The Sovereign Lord has given me a well-instructed tongue, to know the word that sustains the weary. He wakens me morning by morning, wakens my ear like one being instructed.' These were the words inscribed inside his bishop's ring, and were pivotal to his understanding of God's call upon his life. Through listening to God, he had been taken back to the basics of his calling. He was given not a new direction but fresh inspiration for an existing one.

At other times, stopping to reflect on our calling can lead to significant change and the sense that it is time to move on to something new. This is sometimes necessary because we can become stale in what we are doing and need a fresh challenge; because we have completed a particular work and God has a new assignment for us; because we need to move on and create space for others to develop their gifts; because we need to keep growing in our faith and be stretched in our discipleship.

Henri Nouwen is one who was brave enough to sense that God had something completely different in store for him. Well known as a priest, writer and academic, Nouwen had been in touch for some time with Jean Vanier, the founder of a community in France (known as L'Arche) for people with learning difficulties. After several short visits to the community, Nouwen began to sense that the restlessness he increasingly felt as a professor at Harvard was, in fact, God's way of leading him somewhere new. In 1985 he resigned his post and went to stay at the community in France for a year. He felt God say to him, 'Go and live among the poor in spirit and they will heal you.'[40]

While he was there, he was invited to become chaplain to the L'Arche community near Toronto in Canada, known as Daybreak. Although it was a struggle for him to decide, eventually he recognised that this was where God wanted him to be, and he accepted the invitation, staying there for the last ten years of his life. The move represented a huge step in what he termed 'downward mobility', the way of Jesus and the servant described in Philippians 2, but it was a move he was happy to make as he sought to do God's will. At Daybreak he found a place of acceptance and healing for himself, just as God had said, and referred to his move there as 'coming home'.

Here we have two people, each with his own story but both living as servants of God, seeking to do his will and glorify him through their lives. They remind us that we are all unique and that God speaks to us as individuals. Each of us has our own race to run and must keep our eyes on Jesus (Hebrews 12:1–2), and, when we take the time to listen to him, we will hear his voice. The most important thing is that we maintain the disposition of a servant and continue to ask the question, 'What do you want to accomplish through me, Lord?' This is a question we can ask for the short-term (today) and for the long-term (the rest of our lives).

Listening and responding are the twin aspects of attentiveness and are the primary qualities of a good servant. Perhaps, as you reach the final paragraph of this book, it is the right time for you to become attentive to God in a very personal way. The question to ask is this: 'What is God saying to me through the Servant Song, and how will I respond?'

Reflection

- Journal your thoughts in response to the above question.
- Spend some time in prayerful reflection on your interaction with this book, going back to the very beginning and reminding yourself of any key passages or truths that have emerged for you as you have worked your way through the Servant Song.

Appendix

These are some characteristics of abusive systems in churches and Christian organisations.

- A leader who is dominating, whose word is law and who does not operate within a genuine plurality of leadership. Such a person may have a strong personality, be exceptionally gifted or be a charismatic figure but is not truly accountable to anyone for their actions.

- A hierarchical power structure where the senior leader is 'king'.

- A strong group identity to which everyone must conform. Loyalty is rewarded by promotion, disloyalty by demotion. There is an inner circle, and people are either in or out of favour according to their degree of conformity.

- A strong sense of elitism—the belief that our group is right and all others are wrong or inferior.

- A climate of intimidation and fear, where questioning is either not allowed or is seen as being awkward. Discussing issues with others may be labelled as gossip.

- High demands being placed on people in terms of their time, resources and energy. Any form of weakness is frowned upon and there is little room for compassion.

- A high degree of control over, for example, who people marry, where they live or what job they do.

- Little room for freedom of conscience or divergence of viewpoint.

- A focus always on the task and seldom on relationships. There is little fun or relaxation, and people appear joyless and unreal.

- A sense that people are expendable and casualties are to be expected.

- People seldom leaving the group peacefully or with blessing. Those who leave may be ostracised.

- Few outside reference points and little by way of genuine accountability. Things are hidden and secret rather than transparent and open. Financial irregularities may occur.

Notes

1. John Finney, *Understanding Leadership* (Daybreak, 1989), p. 47.
2. Richard Foster, *Celebration of Discipline* (Hodder & Stoughton, 1980), p. 115.
3. Foster, *Celebration of Discipline*, p. 102.
4. Henri Blocher, *Songs of the Servant* (Regent College Publishing, 2005), p. 59.
5. Blocher, *Songs of the Servant*, p. 73.
6. John Stott, *The Preacher's Portrait* (Tyndale Press, 1961), p. 94.
7. Brian Kolodiejchuk, *Come Be My Light* (Rider, 2008), p. 291.
8. Roger Steer, *Inside Story* (IVP, 2009), p. 161.
9. Richard Stearns, *The Hole in the Gospel* (Thomas Nelson, 2009), p. 238.
10. Stearns, *Hole in the Gospel*, p. 10.
11. Robert K. Greenleaf, *Servant Leadership* (Paulist Press, 1977), p. 13.
12. Greenleaf, *Servant Leadership*, pp. 13–14.
13. Finney, *Understanding Leadership*, p. 45.
14. Dan R. Ebener, *Servant Leadership Models for your Parish* (Paulist Press, 2010), p. 33.
15. Duane Elmer, *Cross-Cultural Servanthood* (IVP, 2006), p. 156.
16. Elmer, *Cross-Cultural Servanthood*, p. 168.
17. Samuel T. Carson, *Songs of the Servant King* (Ambassador, 2001), p. 43.
18. Quoted by C.J. Mahaney, *Humility: True Greatness* (Multnomah, 2006), p. 29.
19. Elmer, *Cross-Cultural Servanthood*, p. 17.
20. Paul Beasley-Murray, *Power for God's Sake* (Paternoster, 1998), pp. 5–6.
21. World Evangelical Alliance, *Worth Keeping* (William Carey Library, 2007), p. 261.
22. C.H. Spurgeon, *Pulpit Legends* (AMG, 1994), pp. 555–556.
23. Alec Motyer, *The Prophecy of Isaiah* (IVP, 1993), p. 320.
24. Henri Nouwen, *Can You Drink the Cup?* (Ave Maria Press, 1996), pp. 36–37.
25. Spurgeon, *Pulpit Legends*, p. 563.
26. Schaeffer Institute, a paper by Dr. Richard Krejcir found at www.intothyword.org/articles and accessed on 19/12/11. [Page has been moved]
27. This is explained more fully in my own book, *Working from a Place of Rest* (BRF, 2010).
28. Paul Tournier, *The Strong and the Weak* (Highland Press, 1984), p. 21.
29. Tan Soo-Inn, *Friends in a Broken World* (Graceworks, 2008), p. 19.

30. Soo-Inn, *Friends in a Broken World*, pp. 2–3.
31. Keith Farmer, quoted in Rick Lewis, *Mentoring Matters* (Monarch, 2009), p. 234.
32. Richard Foster, *Money, Sex and Power* (Hodder & Stoughton 1985), p. 1.
33. Farmer, in Lewis, *Mentoring Matters*, pp. 234–235.
34. Derek Tidball, *Wisdom from Heaven* (Christian Focus, 2003), p. 23.
35. Dave Kraft, *Leaders Who Last* (Crossway, 2010), p. 12.
36. Alan Jamieson, *Chrysalis* (Paternoster, 2007), p. 78.
37. Rick Warren, *The Purpose-Driven Life* (Zondervan, 2002), pp. 17–18.
38. Warren, *Purpose Driven Life*, p. 57.
39. Ken Clarke, *Going for Growth* (IVP, 2011), pp. 145–146.
40. Henri Nouwen, *In the Name of Jesus* (DLT, 1989), p. 11.

Bibliography

On the Servant Songs:
Henri Blocher, *Songs of the Servant* (Regent College Publishing, 2005)
Samuel T. Carson, *Songs of the Servant King* (Ambassador, 2001)
Alec Motyer, *The Prophecy of Isaiah* (IVP, 1993)

On servanthood in general:
Eddie Gibbs, *Way to Serve* (IVP, 2003)
Duane Elmer, *Cross-Cultural Servanthood* (IVP, 2006)
Ajith Fernando, *An Authentic Servant* (IFES, 2006)
Charles Swindoll, *Improving Your Serve* (Hodder & Stoughton, 1981)

On issues of justice:
Gary Haugen, *Good News about Injustice* (IVP, 2009)
Timothy Keller, *A Generous Justice* (Hodder & Stoughton, 2010)
Richard Stearns, *The Hole in the Gospel* (Thomas Nelson, 2009)

On character:
Pamela Evans, *Shaping the Heart* (BRF, 2011)
Richard Foster, *Celebration of Discipline* (Hodder & Stoughton, 1980)
Richard Foster, *Money, Sex and Power* (Hodder & Stoughton, 1985)
C.J. Mahaney, *Humility: True Greatness* (Multnomah, 2006)
Andrew Murray, *Humility* (Whitaker House, 1982)
Richard Sibbes, *The Bruised Reed* (Banner of Truth, 2000)
Tan Soo-Inn, *Friends in a Broken World* (Graceworks, 2008)
C.Peter Wagner, *Humility* (Regal Books, 2002)

On servant-leadership:
Ken Blanchard & Phil Hodges, *Lead Like Jesus* (Thomas Nelson, 2005)

Dan R Ebener, *Servant Leadership Models for Your Parish* (Paulist Press, 2010)

John Finney, *Understanding Leadership* (Daybreak, 1989)

Robert K. Greenleaf, *Servant Leadership* (Paulist Press, 1977)

Denny Gunderson, *The Leadership Paradox* (YWAM, 2006)

Dave Kraft, *Leaders Who Last* (Crossway, 2010)

J. David Lundy, *Servant Leadership* (Authentic, 2002)

Tom Marshall, *Understanding Leadership* (Sovereign World, 1991)

Calvin Miller, *The Empowered Leader* (Broadman & Holman, 1995)

Henri Nouwen, *In the Name of Jesus* (DLT, 1989)

Stephen Prosser, *To Be a Servant Leader* (Paulist Press, 2007)

Simon Walker, *The Undefended Leader* (Piquant, 2007)

C. Gene Wilkes, *Jesus on Leadership* (Tyndale House, 1998)

Walter C. Wright, *Relational Leadership* (Paternoster, 2000)

Questions for group discussion

Please read the appropriate chapter beforehand. Use the questions to help you understand the subject matter more fully, and the discussion to take your thoughts further in personal and group application.

Chapter 1
Read Isaiah 42:1–7.

- Does your attention wander easily? Do you find that you are often distracted from looking at Jesus? What draws you away from him?
- Do you have any negative thoughts about servanthood? Why do you think Jesus took the form of a servant? What does this say to you?
- Consider each of the three expressions of the word 'Behold'. Try to keep them in mind as you read the book. Write or share a prayer as you begin this journey of interaction with the Servant Song.

Chapter 2
Read Philippians 2:5–11.

- In what ways does Jesus perfectly demonstrate the role of a servant?
- How are we to understand the fact that he 'emptied' himself? How does his example challenge his followers today?
- In what ways did Jesus 'humble' himself? How does Paul apply this teaching to the church at Philippi, and how might it apply to our lives?

Chapter 3
Read John 13:1–17.

- In what sense was Jesus 'chosen' by the Father? What did this mean to him?
- How did the Father show his delight in the Son? Why did Jesus need to hear such words of affirmation and love?
- What do you think we learn from the washing of the disciples' feet?

Chapter 4
Read Mark 9:33–37.

- What does it mean that we are to walk in the steps of Jesus (1 John 2:6; 1 Peter 2:21)?
- What can we learn from the terms *doulos* and *diakonos*? How are they similar and how are they different?
- How might things change in your church or organisation if everyone saw themselves as a servant of God? How is servant-hood being expressed in your life?

Chapter 5
Read Ephesians 5:15–20.

- Why are human energy, zeal and enthusiasm inadequate when it comes to doing the will of God?
- Why does the servant welcome the help of the Spirit? How did the Spirit help Jesus in his earthly ministry?
- What do we learn here about the Trinity and the relationship between Father, Son and Spirit? What does this teach us about our relationships?
- How would you answer the question 'Are you serving in dependency upon the Spirit?'

Chapter 6
Read Isaiah 53:1–12.

- Why is justice an important part of the servant's ministry?
- How does the cross demonstrate both the justice and the love of God? Why did the servant have to become a *suffering* servant?
- What are the results of justification, and what impact have they had on your life? Why must the church continue to preach 'Christ and him crucified' (1 Corinthians 1:22)?

Chapter 7
Read Luke 4:16–21.

- Why does true religion have a moral content and a social conscience?
- How did Jesus champion the cause of the poor? How did he demonstrate compassion?
- 'Grace should make us just.' Why are some believers nervous about social involvement? How might we answer their concerns?
- Reflect on the stories of Richard Stearns and Mei Ling. Is there a 'hole' in your gospel?

Chapter 8
Read Mark 10:35–45.

- How do you respond to the assertion that character is more important than gifting?
- Christian leadership is *servant* leadership. What do you understand by this term? How does it affect the way we lead?
- What are some common reservations or misunderstandings about servant-leadership? How can these concerns be answered?
- Why should we serve first and lead second?

Chapter 9
Read 1 Peter 5:1–7.

- Have you ever been aware of pride in your own life? Why is it considered a deadly sin?
- Humility is the key characteristic of the servant and is seen supremely in Jesus. How can we define or describe humility?
- Consider each of the three manifestations of pride: self-display, aggressive defensiveness and self-determination. How do true servants counteract these human tendencies?
- Reflect on the saying of John Stott that pride is our greatest enemy and humility our greatest friend.

Chapter 10
Read Matthew 12:15–21.

- How does the way we treat people reveal what is in our hearts? Why is it vital to have a balance between power and compassion?
- What do you understand by the terms 'a bruised reed' and 'a smouldering flax'?
- Why is power often not handled well in churches and Christian organisations? What is the difference between strong visionary leadership and that which is abusive or manipulative?
- Reflect on the words of Jesus: 'I am among you as one who serves' (Luke 22:27).

Chapter 11
Read Hebrews 12:1–3.

- Have you ever been tempted to give up? What happened, and how did you keep going?
- What challenges did Jesus face? How did he resource himself to remain faithful despite all that he suffered?
- What do you consider to be 'the cost of discipleship'? How can we develop greater resilience within ourselves as we follow Jesus? What confidence can we have that we will make it to the end?

Chapter 12
Read Isaiah 55:8–11.

- Have you seen for yourself the difference that confidence can make to a person, whatever their walk in life?
- How do you respond to the statistics about people in ministry in America?
- Identify the three confidence-building promises in Isaiah 42: 6–7. Why is it significant that they are made by the Creator God? What does it mean that his word has both creative and sustaining power?
- How may God speak to encourage us? How has he spoken words that have encouraged you?

Chapter 13
Read 2 Timothy 4:16–18.

- What is the significance of being called in righteousness?
- How do we become aware of the divine presence, and how does the nearness of God strengthen us? Why is loneliness and isolation a particular challenge to us all? How might you allow God to take your hand?
- What can we learn from the story of Tan-Soo Inn? Where might you find spiritual friendship?

Chapter 14
Read Psalm 121.

- Are you aware that Satan wants to render God's servants in-effective? Have you experienced this personally? Have you seen it in the lives of others?
- Consider each of the three main battlegrounds for temptation— money, sex and power. How can we protect ourselves in each area? Reflect on the five steps described in 1 Corinthians 10:12– 13.

- What forms might trials take, and how can they destabilise our faith? How do we resource ourselves in times of testing? What are some of the beneficial outcomes if we endure?

Chapter 15
Read Philippians 2:12–18.

- Why does inner transformation lead to greater outer effectiveness?
- How does God work in us to shape our character? What is he seeking to do? How can we know if we are becoming more Christ-like? Share your thoughts on the six aspects of inner transformation.
- Why is it important that we grow in our competency in ministry? Where does our confidence come from? What does it mean to be an 'instrument in the hand of God'?
- What can we learn from the example of the couple working in Africa?

Chapter 16
Read Isaiah 50:4–9.

- Why is attentiveness (listening and responding) an essential quality for a servant?
- How do we give glory to God? Why is it so fiercely contested?
- When you look back on your history with God (as an individual or as a group), what can you learn?
- As you think about the future, what do you sense God is saying to you—confirming what you are already doing or calling you to something new?
- How has God spoken to you through the Servant Song, and how will you respond?